The Truth Doesn't Have to Hurt

The Truth Doesn't Have to Hurt

How to Use Criticism to Strengthen Relationships, Improve Performance, and Promote Change

DEB BRIGHT

⁴AMACOM

American Management Association
New York • Atlanta • Brussels • Chicago • Mexico City •
San Francisco • Shanghai • Tokyo • Toronto • Washington, D.C.

Bulk discounts available. For details visit:
www.amacombooks.org/go/specialsales
Or contact special sales:
Phone: 800-250-5308
Email: specialsls@amanet.org
View all the AMACOM titles at: www.amacombooks.org
American Management Association: www.amanet.org

This publication is designed to provide accurate and authoritative information in regard to the subject matter covered. It is sold with the understanding that the publisher is not engaged in rendering legal, accounting, or other professional service. If legal advice or other expert assistance is required, the services of a competent professional person should be sought.

Library of Congress Cataloging-in-Publication Data

Bright, Deborah.
 The truth doesn't have to hurt : how to use criticism to strengthen relationships, improve performance, and promote change / Deb Bright.
    pages cm
  Includes index.
  ISBN-13: 978-0-8144-3481-9 (pbk.)
  ISBN-10: 0-8144-3481-9 (pbk.)
  ISBN-13: 978-0-8144-3482-6 (ebook)
 1. Criticism, Personal. 2. Interpersonal relations. 3. Performance. 4. Change (Psychology)
I. Title.
  BF637.C74B753 2015
  158.2--dc23
                    2014020765

About AMA
American Management Association (www.amanet.org) is a world leader in talent development, advancing the skills of individuals to drive business success. Our mission is to support the goals of individuals and organizations through a complete range of products and services, including classroom and virtual seminars, webcasts, webinars, podcasts, conferences, corporate and government solutions, business books, and research. AMA's approach to improving performance combines experiential learning—learning through doing—with opportunities for ongoing professional growth at every step of one's career journey.

Printing number

10 9 8 7 6 5 4 3 2 1

Contents

Acknowledgments

The impetus for writing this book would not have been possible without the initial support and contribution of Dr. Mark Pochapin, founder of the Jay Monahan Center in New York. Together we began what ultimately resulted in a seven-year journey that finally culminated in the Strategies for Enhancing Performance Study, which became the foundation of the research upon which much of this book is based.

What we learned from surveying over a thousand workers in the Northeast is that criticism, whether as a giver or receiver, is among the top ten most stressful factors affecting performance in workplaces. While exchanges involving negative feedback do not occur all the time in the average worker's day, when they do, they are stress-producing.

The Strategies for Enhancing Performance Study itself, and the many subsequent journal articles on it that followed, would not have been possible without the participants who engaged in the experimental control design study. A special thank you goes out to those organizations and companies who participated in this effort. They include: Aetna, Banker's Life and Casualty, Executive Women's Golf Association (EWGA), GE Healthcare, Hadassah, the Ladies Professional Golf Association (LPGA), Morgan Stanley, NAI Horizons, New York Association of Homes and Services for the Aging (NYAHSA), New York Hilton Hotel, NYSE Euronext, and the University Medical Center (UMC). It was through the employees' participation that we learned what skills in today's workplace lend themselves to improving performance while simultaneously mitigating the negative effects of stress.

I also want to express my thanks to Dan Manship for sticking with me throughout the process of writing this book. The researching and subsequent documentation, along with the arduous task of inputting the material, took a lot of work on his part and it is greatly appreciated. Thanks for making sure the book's message was clear and moved along smoothly goes to David Gould and his great editorial skills. Karen Moraghan from Hunter Publications also deserves a thank you because she introduced me to David and was so helpful in the promotion of the book.

Naturally, the book would not have happened if it weren't for my most helpful and dedicated agent, Katie Kotchman, of whose encouragement and persistence I am most grateful. Her conscientiousness and belief in the subject was all inspiring. It was through Katie that I met Ellen Kadin, my talented editor at AMACOM. Ellen is a person whose main talents are motivation mixed with inspiration and kindness. I thank her and greatly respect her for her spot on advice and for always being so easily accessible. Working with Ellen, Erika Spelman, Irene Majuk, and all the enthusiastic staff at AMACOM was a pleasure, and I wouldn't hesitate to do it all over again!

Also, thanks needs to go out to the women at WATT (Women at the Top). This is a group of highly successful Tucson, Arizona, entrepreneurs and business executives who are at the top of their game, whose opinions I respect without question and whom I have come to like personally.

A special thank you also needs to be extended to Penelope Boehm, President of Boehm Business Services, a good friend and successful business owner, for her help with surveying Toastmasters members.

And most important, a very special thank you goes to my husband, Paul. He is my best friend, my lover, my confidant, and my most cherished critic. He was so helpful in stimulating thought and making sure that what was written was well thought-out and would stand the test of time.

A final thank you goes to all of those individuals in the workplace today who understand criticism and the vital role it plays in enhancing performance and building quality relationships and bringing about change. It's those believers I want to thank because they understand that the goal is not to promote more criticism in the workplace today . . . rather it is to engage in helpful criticism exchanges because only when we do that can individuals realize their full potential and organizations maintain their competitive edge.

The Truth
Doesn't Have
to Hurt

Introduction

> *The trouble with most of us is that we would rather be ruined by praise than saved by criticism.*[1]
>
> —NORMAN VINCENT PEALE

S tanding 10 meters above the earth, balancing on the edge of a diving platform, I would listen to my coach yelling corrective instructions about what I needed to do to make my next dive better. Most people would consider his harsh admonishments mixed with encouragement as criticism, but for me, it was direction, instruction, and insight. Through training and a plentiful amount of no-holds-barred criticism from him, I was able to exceed even my own expectations as a diver. Because I accepted his criticisms as helpful, I eventually became ranked among the top ten women divers in the United States. Unfortunately, my career in platform and springboard Olympic competition ended suddenly when doctors discovered retinal tears in both my eyes. Had I continued, I was told, blindness would have been the inevitable result.

Initially, I was devastated by the loss of my Olympic dreams. I was determined, however, not to let my years of training experience go to waste, so I used my knowledge in competitive diving as the foundation for starting my career in the area of improving others' individual performance. In the years that followed, I emerged as a nationally recognized expert in the fields of criticism, stress management, communication skills, and leadership development.

CRITICISM, STRESS, AND JOB PERFORMANCE

Research initiated by our office, Bright Learning Enterprises, resulted in a national study that ran from 2003 to 2010 and led to some significant findings on the relationship between stress and criticism. These findings were compiled and formed a workplace program we called Strategies for Enhancing Performance Study and Program. The goal was to understand the power of criticism and the best ways that individuals could use criticism for positive change. The skills that were introduced in the study have been proved to yield consistent positive results among study participants.

I conducted other national studies on criticism with Simmons Market Research Bureau, which led to my writing two books about criticism. Now, I lecture around the world on the subject, and I have designed licensed training programs for some of the most prestigious organizations in the United States. Rather than calling myself an executive coach or consultant, I jokingly refer to myself as an "insultant." Though being an Olympian was not in my stars, as it turned out, I did gain a kind of blue-ribbon expertise when it came to the three sides of criticism: giving criticism, receiving criticism, and the silent destructor—self-criticism.

Findings from the Strategies for Enhancing Performance Study show that being on the receiving end of criticism and having to give criticism rank among the top ten most stress-producing challenges in the workplace. When asked, most people declare that they are not proficient at handling criticism. How about you? Can you think of the last time you were criticized by your boss, your mate, your friend, or maybe even your kids? How did you respond? Were you hurt, upset, or even angry? When it comes to criticism, the awful

The Strategies for Enhancing Performance Study

The Strategies for Enhancing Performance Study, its results, and the skill sets and techniques used are mentioned frequently in this book. The following is a brief background of that study.

Launched in 2003, Phase I of the study consisted of surveying more than one thousand working people in the Northeast for the purpose of identifying the most effective behavioral and cognitive skills, or Performance Control Practices, used to enhance performance and mitigate the negative effects of stress.

Phase II then followed, in which 320 professionals from a wide range of industries (e.g., healthcare, finance) participated in an experimental/control design study. Participants in the experimental group engaged in a learning seminar where we introduced the ten most effective Performance Control Practices identified from Phase I of the study. The experimental group also completed an individualized Performance Control Plan and received a follow-up thirty-minute tele-coaching call. Participants in the control group received none of this training.

After both the experimental and control groups completed pre- and posttest questionnaires, comparisons between the two groups showed significant differences in a number of key areas. A few of them include:

► Improvement in job satisfaction and performance

► Ability to rebound effectively from setbacks and disappointments

► Greater effectiveness when on the receiving end of criticism

► Greater effectiveness at giving another person criticism

► Greater effectiveness at leaving "work problems" at the office

► Ability to overcome the negative effects of stress by identifying solutions to issues that positively impact work and articulating ideas clearly and concisely

For additional insights into the results, and to learn more about the Strategies for Enhancing Performance Study, check out the October 2011 issue of *Nursing Management* and the January 2012 issue of *Coaching: An International Journal of Theory, Research and Practice.*

truth is that it takes only a few words or maybe just a perceived frown of disapproval to create a drama that has the potential to jeopardize or, in time, even destroy an important relationship. In fact, through my research, it was found that more than any other form of communication, criticism has the potential power to fatally ruin relationships. Nevertheless, as diligently as we might try to avoid it, criticism is inescapable and inevitably plays a major role in shaping our lives. If we are to succeed as parents, employees, leaders, or players, it is critical that we learn how to deal with criticism as both givers and receivers.

If you are a CEO or an executive and wish to promote open communication in your organization, then criticism plays a powerful role in what it means to operate in an environment of openness. Just as organizations need to be effective at problem solving, decision making, handling change, and recognizing and rewarding their employees, they also need to be skillful at handling criticism. Organizations that do not skillfully address criticism are breeding grounds for mediocre outcomes and low morale.

THE SKILL OF HANDLING CRITICISM AS A GIVER OR RECEIVER

If you are in HR, you are obviously concerned about recent trends in employee attitudes regarding respect for supervisors and organizational loyalty, not to mention the implications associated with the verbal misconduct that often accompanies this lack of respect. If these trends gain momentum in the business community, HR departments will need to standardize approaches for how employees handle feedback, much the same way HR addresses workplace violence and sexual harassment. If you are a leader, how can you help employees grow and develop, and how can you hold people accountable, without understanding criticism and being skilled as both a giver and a receiver?

As an employee, understanding criticism and being skillful in both giving and receiving it, as well as handling self-criticism, is imperative to your growth and development if you wish to be successful in your pursuits. That is the reason I wrote this book. My hope is that your relationships as well as your ambitions can grow stronger and be better enhanced when you learn the techniques I write about here.

Are you a candidate for this book? Consider the following:

- At work, has your leadership emphasized the need for more open communication and transparency?

- Does your company or organization conduct performance reviews or utilize 360° instruments?

- In the last thirty days, has your boss given you some negative feedback, or has a peer reproached you for not doing something that you promised? Have you recently been told that you have failed to live up to certain expectations?

- Are you frustrated because you believe you are not getting the kind of assignments that you think you are qualified to handle?

- Do you think that the reason you are not being promoted has more to do with lack of office popularity than lack of talent or expertise?

- Is gaining respect from your colleagues and supervisors important to you, yet frustratingly difficult?

If you answered "yes" to any of these questions, then you may very well be overlooking an important skill set to add to your repertoire of tools. You could most certainly benefit from reading this book.

Likewise, from an organizational perspective:

- Are you interested in promoting a helpful workplace where employees learn from one another and have a sincere desire to create an environment where open communication prevails?

► Would you prefer to work in an environment where there's no need to second-guess one another, especially when compliments or praise is delivered, as well as when corrective suggestions and advice are offered?

► Would you like it if peers and coworkers were encouraged to admit mistakes up front instead of blaming others and making excuses?

Once again, if you answered "yes" to any of these questions, then what you will learn from this book is imperative because understanding criticism, combined with being skilled as a giver and receiver of it, enables you and your coworkers to operate in a helpful workplace.

THE UNAVOIDABILITY OF CRITICISM IN OUR LIVES

What's interesting about criticism is that it doesn't end in the workplace; it's alive and well off the job among family members and friends. One mother recently confided to me that she had to have a heart-to-heart conversation with her daughter. The daughter, a newlywed, had failed to take a strong stand over her new husband's careless spending habits. It was extremely difficult for the mother to approach her daughter because there had never before been a need to discuss money issues. Yet, it was becoming unbearable for her to see her daughter succumb to her husband's spending frenzy and say nothing about it. What really prompted the conversation for the mother was the reality that her own husband—the major family breadwinner—was now out of work, and the family was less able to bail the daughter out financially as they had in the past.

Besides those big issues where criticism becomes imperative, there are also the everyday criticisms that need to be dealt with among family members. Among them, for instance, are things not being put away properly, lights not being turned off, or someone saying something with a sharp tone of voice at the wrong time. Or there's having to deal with friends who don't return borrowed items, who gossip about you, who show up late to an event, or who cancel at the last minute, ruining your best-laid plans. Whether the issues are big or small, loaded with drama or without, the need for occasional criticism is all around us! You can be sure about one thing: To postpone or avoid saying something in the hope that the situation will go away is almost never the solution!

So far, we have been talking about face-to-face interactions involving criticism. However, there are also all the new technologies we have today in our communications outlets. When it comes to criticism, the instant you press "send" can result in consequences that can seriously alter your aspirations and relationships. Texting, social media, and email can be dangerous tools of communication if you happen to be one of the growing number of people who are impatient and react quickly. How many times have you hit the send button only to wish that you had not done so? Before, we had "speak first and regret it later," but now we have compounded our stress because we can also "send (or text) first, regret it, and regret it, and regret it!" To our dismay, all these communications are archived!

Most of us can recall some degree of etiquette training we received from our parents, teachers, and religious leaders as we were growing up. We learned the importance of showing gratitude to those who were kind to us and were encouraged to minimize our hostility to those who were not so kind. We learned the appropriateness of when to say "thank you" and "please" as well as when to give praise. We were told that such social expectations were part of our culture and how we deal with others. But how much training have we really had on the subject of criticism? Were we ever told that criticism is inevitable? Did anyone explain to us the unexpected consequences it might have for our relationships if handled poorly? Dealing with criticism in a productive manner is a skill, whether we are on the receiving end or the giving end. And yet, these are not skills that get handed down or come to us intuitively. Parents—like most anyone else—are generally unschooled in and unaware of such skills as they apply to bringing up children or dealing with relatives.

Very little training on criticism occurs in college management courses or workplace seminars. Colleges and business organizations offer courses on presentation skills because they are necessary in the workplace. So, too, is it necessary to learn the skills of giving and receiving criticism. Once these skills are learned, criticism has the power to become one of the most consequential tools in our arsenal for creating motivation, trust, and respect with all the people we deal with—be they friends, employees, children, parents, competitors, or enemies. Why? Because, unlike praise, criticism is always perceived as truth unless it is merely or obviously intended to hurt. Understanding how to sort out helpful criticism or criticism that is intended to improve performance (as opposed to any other kind of criticism) is what you will learn in this book.

THE GOAL OF THIS BOOK

The goal of this book is to give you the tools you need to live a confident life, where you won't be intimidated or fearful about giving or receiving criticism. This will be accomplished by teaching you the key skills behind delivering and receiving helpful criticism. As the giver, you'll learn how to deliver criticism so it is received as you intended and you have the best chance of having it accepted with appreciation. As the receiver, you'll learn how to avoid personalizing it and how you can benefit from helpful criticism. Once you have absorbed this book, you will be able to deliver criticism that will give you the results you want. You will have the confidence to receive criticism from others, and you will be able to control your own self-defeating criticism with the simple application of a few basic skills.

Like most of us, you may have lived your life clueless as to the inherent power of criticism. After learning the skills taught in this book, you will live the rest of your life with a clear understanding of how to give and receive criticism so that it empowers you and actually enriches your relationships with others.

PART ONE

Understanding the Power and Use of Criticism

CHAPTER 1

Criticism Doesn't Have to Hurt

> *Criticism may not be agreeable, but it is necessary. It fulfills the same function as pain in the human body. It calls attention to an unhealthy state of things.*[1]
>
> —WINSTON CHURCHILL

Picture yourself in an audience of a few hundred people. The speaker behind the podium opens her presentation with the following question: "How many of you enjoy being criticized?" Would you raise your hand? If you are anything like the audience of four hundred people who were asked this question at a recent corporate retreat in Sarasota, Florida, your hand would have stayed down. Surprisingly, there were a few hands that went up. The speaker asked each person to explain. As it turned out, those who had raised their hands were at one time either athletes or involved in the arts. They said they saw criticism as a way of becoming better at what they do. But each of them was quick to say that there were only a few people, such as their coaches and instructors, whom they considered eligible to criticize them. The audience spontaneously burst into unexpected applause followed by some chatter, as if to suggest an "aha" moment of great understanding.

What is it among the majority of us that is really behind all the resistance and discomfort associated with criticism? The likely answer is that criticism, by its nature, is usually considered a negative stimulus with the power to create a strong reaction or perhaps even an emotional outburst.

OUR CULTURAL ATTITUDES TOWARD CRITICISM

Western culture's social sensitivity to criticism is all around us. Some corporate HR departments and school officials have difficulty with the very word "criticism." Some great companies have people in influential roles who discourage use of the word because they consider it too harsh or negative. Discomfort with the term itself has led organizations to mask it by calling it "constructive criticism," "negative feedback," "appreciative feedback," "constructive feedback," and other synonymous words that remove some of the negative sting. A telecommunications company in the Midwest called it "caring confrontation." That's not bad, but whether it's taken as "caring" or not remains up to the person who is receiving it! No matter what they call it, organizations interested in improving the performance and efficiencies of their ranks understand the necessity of criticism and its importance in the employee evaluation process. These same organizations are also aware of the inherent dangers related to criticism that is poorly delivered by supervisors to the workers under them.

To avoid tracing the individual source of an evaluation, many organizations resort to the use of 360° instruments, which use a limited set of questions to provide anonymous feedback from a work-associated group to an individual. Typically done on an annual basis, use of these instruments often involves the participation of subordinates and bosses or other high-level people as well as peers. Sometimes customers provide input. And it is that surrounding population that makes it 360°. Criticism coming out of such evaluations can often be helpful. However, because the observations and comments are anonymous, they can wind up being used by some to make deliberate accusations without fear of reprisal or direct confrontation. Often, what results is a mystery hunt of who said what about whom, which can get in the way of any meaningful information useful to those on the receiving end.

When applying 360°'s, receivers get generalized comments that can often wind up leaving them with accusations that they may or may not think are accurate. Furthermore, receivers are often left clueless about what they need to do to correct their behavior. What can be even more troubling is whether the receiver's boss regards the anonymous information as important to the employee's standing and career in the organization. So while the intent of 360°'s may have been to be helpful, their reliability can easily be faulty, and they can be used in a debilitating and manipulative way. Poorly managed 360° evaluative methods are fraught with potentially damaging effects on receivers because they invite skepticism, which doesn't promote a helpful and healthy workplace atmosphere.

There can be little doubt that criticism's negative cultural stigma has fostered a societal antipathy toward this powerful and potentially helpful communication tool. When randomly asking people their thoughts about criticism, most everyone describes it as something negative. Because it is misused by the majority of us, who have never learned how to use it effectively, we have come to regard it as a blatant form of impoliteness even though we know that there are times and situations when it is necessary and would even help people to become better at what they do or how they interact with others. Most people associate the word with personal bashing and being hurtful. A few people even associate criticism with outright bullying. Some simply view it as the opposite of praise. One blogger exemplified clearly the confusion that exists today when she said she would rather receive "feedback" than "criticism." Whether in the workplace or in schools, if there is any training on criticism, it is often on the handling of "difficult" or "crucial" conversations, "avoiding conflicts," and "delivering negative feedback" to address performance-related issues. These synonymic platitudes do little to advance the true positive power inherent in criticism and instead minimize the fact that fundamentally it is a skill that must be learned by givers and especially receivers. The lack of understanding about criticism is seen within business and industry, where leaders and trainers all too often dismiss the need to train their employees in how to be helpful givers and receptive receivers.

The problem for most of us with all this negativity about using criticism is that criticizing someone now challenges our scruples, which are those internal instincts or considerations. We know in our heart that they are the right things to do, but we often hesitate to do them because we fear the results. Not educating people in the effective use of criticism is a major oversight if organizations want to uphold standards in order to remain competitive and promote a "helpful" environment where performance, efficiencies, and careers are truly enhanced.

While it may seem reasonable to be uncomfortable with criticism, this discomfort actually comes from people's unawareness of how to properly use this powerful tool. For most of us, our approach too often lacks preparation, and the results can be devastating. This holds true across the board, from parents criticizing their children to managers criticizing their employees. Throughout the workplace, being seen as a positive person can be as important as being fashionably dressed. It doesn't take much in the current work environment for someone to be labeled a "naysayer," a "grumpy old man," or a "critical person." If you are a female, you could easily be labeled a "bitch." Better to be a "team player." All too often, that means going along with group consensus, regardless of personal convictions. Such attitudes may enhance popularity, but they do little to effect real positive changes.

Believe it or not, it is quite possible to be viewed as a supportive, trustworthy, and valuable team player even though you do engage in criticizing others when you deem it appropriate. It all has to do with your purpose for giving the criticism and then packaging your message in such a way that the receiver sees it as helpful and having their best interest in mind. By always keeping the intent behind your criticism helpful, you ensure that no one will ever think of you as anything less than a supportive friend and cherished team player. The fact is that most of us have never learned how to effectively employ criticism, and we are simply not effective in giving it.

CRITICISM CAN BE HELPFUL

The word "criticism" derives from the Greek word *kritikos*, which means "able to judge or discern." The dictionary tells us that criticism means "the expression of disapproval of someone or something based on perceived faults or mistakes" or "the act of passing judgment." While these definitions have validity, they fall short of grasping the true and beneficial complexities of criticism and the intentions behind it. Sometimes criticism is meant to help, and sometimes it's meant to be hurtful. We need to reach out for the motivation behind it before we make any judgments or conclusions regarding our rejection or acceptance.

It's important to realize that criticism doesn't have to be just about correcting someone's behavior or attitude, nor does it always have to be directed at bad behavior. At times, criticism can be delivered to help someone who's doing something well do it even better. A young sales representative, for instance, who has lots of potential to go places in his organization reported that he was approached by his boss after delivering a dynamite sales presentation. He was told that he never once smiled throughout his pitch and that his talk contained a number of bothersome misstatements. The sales rep viewed his boss's observations as helpful tips that he appreciated hearing because he was totally unaware of these things. Consider athletes, artists, dancers, writers, and the like: They may have achieved great heights in their careers, but they still are seeking guidance to improve their abilities.

Whether at work or at home, among loved ones, friends, and coworkers, be they young or old, educated or not, male or female, criticism is all around us, and it often contains hints or outright eye-openers of better ways we can achieve our goals and our ambitions. But we must learn to recognize whether it is meant to hurt or help us. Poorly delivered criticism—or anything other than what this book calls "helpful criticism"—has no merits and should be discouraged by givers and ignored by receivers.

Giving helpful criticism is a skill that needs to be learned before it can be properly understood as "helpful criticism" to the one receiving it. For helpful criticism to result in positive outcomes, there must exist the ingredient of positive intent from the standpoint of the giver and the receiver. It takes two to do this tango. The criticism exchange shifts quickly like dance steps and involves a give-and-take aspect. With each move, perceptions change with regard to the interactions and objectives of what actually is in play. In a back-and-forth exchange of criticism, exactly who is really in control of the process switches. To even begin unraveling the exchange and to understand the power of criticism, it is important to realize that it's the receiver of criticism, not the giver, who is actually in control. This is a key point: Even though you may be giving the criticism, you are not the one in control. The receiver is in control of the process, for it is the receiver who can accept or reject it. There is more about this important point later in this chapter.

Why shouldn't we consider "helpful criticism" as simply synonymous with "constructive criticism"? There is really no good reason why we can't. But the adjective "helpful" sounds a lot less onerous and requires less reflection between givers and receivers than "constructive" does. With the word "helpful" we don't have to go very far to examine what is said or meant in order to divine its intent. It's either helpful or it's not. "Constructive," on the other hand, does not quite hit the comfortable sounding note that "helpful" does, especially to receivers. Using the words "constructive criticism" when giving criticism can seem to some that it's part of an ongoing building process or a kind of master-student didactic session—the true goal of which a receiver may eventually come to understand. It's kind of like when you were a kid, your mother might have said, "Take the medicine, and if you don't like it, hold your nose, 'cause it's good for you—you'll see."

As for praise, we all like praise and we've seen the way it can encourage people. Our observations are backed up scientifically by Abraham Maslow, Frederick Herzberg, and other motivational theorists who addressed praise as a motivator while making very little reference to the value of criticism. Some writers refrain from recognizing the use of criticism as a motivational tool. For instance, Dale Carnegie's *How* to *Win Friends and Influence People* informs the reader: "Criticism is dangerous, because it wounds a person's precious pride, hurts his sense of importance, and arouses resentment."[2] Carnegie wasn't talking about helpful criticism. He was talking about poorly delivered criticism that contains unhelpful intentions.

BOTH CRITICISM AND PRAISE CAN BE VIEWED AS MOTIVATORS

What would happen in the workplace if a manager relied exclusively on praise? Over time, such an approach would lose value and mean very little to those receiving it. Why? We all know we are not perfect, and praise that is not offset once in a while by criticism becomes not only unconvincing but downright suspect. A steady diet of applause is bound to give us a distorted view of who we are in relationship to the true value we bring to an organization. Finally, the overuse of praise creates an inevitability that performance standards become lower than is desirable—something potentially devastating to an organization competing in the global market. After all, when we praise someone, what are we really saying? The simple translation is: "You're doing a great job. Keep up the good work." Was there any room left for performing at a higher level? Praise doesn't necessarily tell us this. Both praise and helpful criticism have much in common, since they both are after the fact, involve judgment, and provide information with the intent to motivate. Where they are different is that criticism implies the need for making a change, whereas praise does not.

A Practical Method for Developing a Praise-to-Criticism Ratio

How much criticism is too much? What's the proper balance between praise and criticism?

You may run across articles that provide specific ratios of praise to criticism—but be cautious about this. Remember, "different strokes for different folks" is one reason against using formulaic approaches. Likewise, the chemistry of individuals makes a tremendous difference as to how one can best deal with another person.

Here's a method that factors in the uniqueness of individuals and the specialness of relationships. Consider the number of interactions you've had with a particular individual over the past thirty days. Now view each of those interactions as snapshot pictures taken from the other person's perspective—as opposed to your own. From the lens of the other person's camera, categorize what percentage each of the interactions falls under:

► Being assigned tasks or being asked for something

► Receiving praise

► Being criticized

If, for example, the individual concludes that the only time you've stopped by or interacted with her was to assign a task or ask for something, that's something to be concerned about. Individuals need to know the outcome of their efforts—whether in the form of praise or criticism.

Likewise, if over the last thirty days most of the contact you've had with this person is to criticize her, then that's not good either. Don't be surprised if the next time you approach her, she cowers or isn't very receptive. This is the time to create opportunities where the person can succeed or to look more closely at what she is doing well and complimenting her for her effort.

Too much criticism isn't good, and neither is too much praise. If you only praise this person, in time you may lose some credibility and, eventually, your effectiveness when dealing with her.

Each person is different, and it's up to you to use your own instincts about the ample use of praise or criticism. You can check out your instincts by casually asking the person directly about whether she thinks you go overboard in either direction.

CRITICISM ISN'T POSITIVE—
BUT IT CAN STILL BE HELPFUL

Criticism at its core will never be positive and never was intended to be. Trying to hide that fact only results in feelings of deception. Take a moment to consider the following words: *advice, recommendation, suggestion, reprimand, complaint, rebuke, chastisement*, and *insult*. What these words have in common is that they are all rooted in some degree of negativity. Where they differ is in their intensity. If we represented these words on a spectrum, it might look something like Figure 1-1.

Figure 1-1.
A SPECTRUM OF WORDS
CONNOTING SOME DEGREE OF CRITICISM

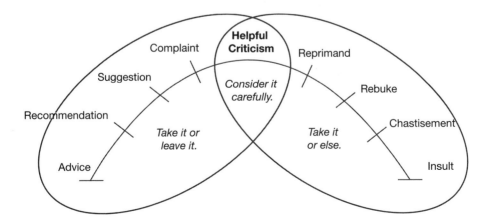

Helpful criticism, or the kind of criticism that is meant to be informative and of benefit, is positioned in the middle of the spectrum. Like advice, recommendation, and suggestion, it is rooted in some degree of negativity. But unlike advice, recommendation, and suggestion, helpful criticism implies the need to bring about a change in behavior. The harsher forms of negativity fall to the right of the spectrum and are depicted with words like *reprimand, rebuke*, and *chastisement*. What is significant about this half of the spectrum is that the expressed disapproval is packaged in accusatory words that rarely leave the person with any option, defense, or recourse.

On the left side of the spectrum, *complaint* is interesting because the negativity associated with it makes it closer to *helpful criticism* than to *reprimand*. While receivers can take or leave a complaint when it comes their way, if ignored or not taken seriously, a complaining customer, for instance, can show control by simply taking business elsewhere—a consequence that well underscores the need to be a good listener who carefully considers what is being said.

GIVING AND RECEIVING
HELPFUL CRITICISM IS A SKILL

Because criticism is always a negative force, it can cause dramatic behavioral changes and other potent responses. This means that we have to be very cautious if we want a good result when we deal with criticism as either a giver or a receiver. Giving helpful criticism is a skill that can easily be learned once we understand the dynamics involved. We must first understand that criticism can be communicated in many ways. It can be a verbal exchange, or it can be a nonverbal exchange consisting of a few words, a simple frown, gazing eyes, or a sigh. It can run the gamut from mild disapproval to the appearance of outrage and disgust.

The good news about helpful criticism is that successfully giving it doesn't require a master's degree in psychology. It's mainly a matter of understanding a process for organizing and presenting your thoughts so they're received as intended and acted upon by the person receiving the criticism. Our goal as givers is to influence change in certain behaviors of receivers. Meanwhile, as receivers, we need to learn the nature of helpful criticism. Once we do, we will understand how to recognize helpful criticism and separate it from other forms of negative input such as insults, demeaning statements, or cutting remarks. Helpful criticism is characteristically instructive criticism at its core. Despite good intentions, however, a giver runs some risk of being perceived by the receiver as hurtful or objectionable.

As we stated earlier, contrary to popular belief, it's the receiver, not the giver, who is in control of the process. All along, most of us have known instinctually that the receiver is in control. Why else would we spend hours mulling over an upcoming conversation involving criticism? When it comes to who controls the criticism process, the perceived power a person such as our boss has over us makes no difference. Just because a boss initiates the criticism makes it tempting for us to think that she is the one who has control during the exchange. However, once the boss or anyone else (be it peers, family members, friends, staff, or mates) delivers the criticism, the receiver can and often does challenge the giver by asking for specific examples. The receiver also decides whether to agree or disagree with the criticism. A receiver who disagrees can reject what the giver is saying and decide not to take any corrective action . . . and that's control! Think about the number of times parents have asked their children to stop texting at a restaurant or stop interrupting when others are speaking. Often, receivers respond with a half-smile and an "okay," only to just walk away. Nevertheless, receivers be warned! Inaction or a wrong reaction to criticism can have consequences.

So where does this leave the boss who gives criticism? Besides being the initiator of the criticism exchange, the boss ultimately assesses the employee's overall performance and the value the employee brings to the organization (during a performance review or similar process where employees are ranked). Bosses need to look at criticism as a tool they can use to create change and as a way to communicate their feelings. In fact, this is true of all givers. They should think of criticism as a dangerously sharp tool that, in the hands of unskilled users, can potentially do damage. But when in the hands of skilled users, it can shape relationships, improve performance, bring about organizational change, and advance trust and respect more than any other communication tool at their disposal.

Criticism is much like pain; though we try to avoid it, it warns us that there is something wrong and we need to take action. As we learned very quickly in childhood, touch a hot pan and we feel pain. If we didn't feel pain, we would burn our flesh. Pain warns us that something negative is happening and we have to do something to change it. When helpful criticism is used effectively, the outcomes are positive. Receivers view the criticism as a valuable learning tool and take steps to use what they have been told for their benefit. Helpful criticism can motivate. Receivers can readily see what they can do better or differently in order to achieve a goal. When givers are properly prepared and receivers are willing to listen to the criticism, relationships between individuals and teams are strengthened. Trust and respect are fostered when people know that there is a willingness to be open and candid with one another. There is no need for second guessing because individuals know that incorrect or undesirable actions will be criticized. Overall performance becomes enhanced and quality results are achieved quicker and at higher levels. Individuals are no longer operating with fear and feeling intimidated by criticism. They know that when they are receiving criticism, it's because the other person has their best interests in mind.

Helpful criticism is a powerful influencer and change catalyst within organizations where employees need to think and operate on the true cutting edge in order for the company to remain competitive. Shifting to a global way of doing business, to focusing on quality, or to emphasizing the need to be more customer-focused or innovative are all examples of where helpful criticism plays a vital role. Helpful criticism is likened to delivering quality information within an organization and conveys what behaviors are acceptable and unacceptable.

COACHING TIP #2

When Criticism Is Perceived as Helpful, People Want More of It

It's been said that public speaking, and specifically having to give a presentation, is one of the greatest fears that we face—especially in business and industry.

One organization that has been known to help people reduce their fears of public speaking is Toastmasters International. Members gain public-speaking skills by practicing in front of other members and then are critiqued or, in their terms, evaluated. When a group of Toastmasters members in the New York City area were surveyed on their thoughts about the evaluations[3] they received from other members, they had the following to say:

► 78 percent of respondents said that the feedback or evaluation they received from other members was either "extremely useful" or "very useful."

► 75 percent of respondents said that, after receiving the feedback, they were either "highly motivated" or "very motivated."

► 84 percent of respondents said that they would be desirous of more honest feedback, even if it was "negative" or "critical."

As this survey reveals, whether in the workplace or as a member of Toastmasters, people really do want helpful criticism! When helpful criticism is given, people are motivated to learn from their mistakes. Wouldn't it be great if your organization developed a culture, like Toastmasters International did, where people seek out helpful criticism in an effort to improve?

RECEIVERS AND GIVERS SHARE RESPONSIBILITY

Regardless of the years of experience we have in a job, when we are around a highly critical person who uses criticism ineffectively, our confidence can easily wobble to the point where we second-guess ourselves. Someone receiving advice, recommendations, or suggestions gets the message that he has the option to take action or not. This is not the case with criticism. When someone is receiving criticism, what's embedded in the message is that he needs to change. This is where many conflicts start.

It reminds me of Bob, a staff member at a major financial company for twenty-plus years. Bob was considered the team's expert on all operational issues, and his former boss relied heavily on Bob's opinion. This wasn't the case, though, with his new boss, Mark. Each day, Mark would micromanage Bob and criticize just about every action that he took. It got to the point where Bob was required to send Mark draft emails about basic office matters before sending them out to his team. Mark would review the emails and point out minor errors. After this happened a few times, Bob shut down. He decided to show up for meetings, say nothing, and do only what he was asked—nothing more. Bob couldn't believe what was happening to his self-confidence and how powerful the effect of Mark's criticism was.

Mark obviously lacked the skills for giving helpful criticism and had no real awareness of Bob's expertise. But Bob never made it a point to inform Mark of this, so Bob's anguish was not necessarily all Mark's fault. When it comes to criticism, as previously said, this tango takes two! From Mark's point of view, his criticisms of Bob may have been intended to help Bob succeed at his job, but Bob's perceptions never took into account that Mark had little or no idea about Bob's talents.

I use this example to show the two fundamental rules for giving and receiving criticism:

1. Givers need to verify that their criticisms are being received as intended and that their intentions are meant to be helpful.

2. Receivers need to ensure that givers are operating with good information and good intentions.

Our culture has drummed into many of our heads that criticism is bad, impolite, and maybe even a violation of someone's human rights or right not to be offended. Can we escape criticism? No chance. It's with us both on and off the job. When we operate with the assumption that human beings aren't perfect, then we are vulnerable to criticism at some point. True, criticism can be harmful, but only if you don't know the basic skills of how to give it and how to receive it. When you learn the techniques in this book, you will go from facing the risk of damaging relationships when speaking candidly to the enlightened place of helpful criticism—where you will experience improved relationships, increased trust and respect, and rewarding outcomes.

Quick Review for Easy Recall

► Criticism is probably the most powerful and assertive form of communication we have at our disposal.

► Criticism and praise have much in common: They both involve judgment, provide information after the fact, and have the intent to motivate.

► Criticism and praise differ in that one is negative and one is positive. Also, criticism implies the need to make a change, where praise does not.

► During an exchange, it's the receiver who is in control. Receivers decide whether or not they agree or disagree with the criticism and if the criticism warrants taking any action.

► With helpful criticism, receivers view the criticism as a valuable learning tool and take steps to use what they have been told for their benefit.

► Giving helpful criticism is a skill that can easily be learned once we understand the dynamics involved.

CHAPTER 2

Criticism Manners

Common Mistakes, and Some Dos and Don'ts

> *A cowardly critique starts with a compliment* [1]
>
> —MOKOKOMA MOKHONOANA

To many people, criticism is the most dreaded form of communication. We very seldom enjoy giving it and basically never enjoy receiving it. This is especially true in times such as now where there is hyperconcern with sensitivity, tolerance, and politeness to others. In such an atmosphere, where does helpful criticism fit in?

Although people overwhelmingly don't like to be corrected, deep down most of us know we sometimes need it. Employees for the most part want to know when they are doing well and when they are not. Effective managers understand that they can't expect employees to improve without being given that kind of information. If you are managing people, providing feedback—be it positive or negative—is essential to individual and team success.

That said, delivering honest feedback can run counter to the keep-things-positive mentality that now prevails. If bosses or, for that matter, employees gain a reputation for being "critical," their message is oftentimes dismissed. No longer seen as "team players," they may find themselves shunned from the core cliques and wind up operating without true support.

CRITICISM AND STRESS GO HAND IN HAND

There is little doubt that giving and receiving criticism are activities that produce stress. To what degree? According to a survey of Northeast workers conducted as part of the Strategies for Enhancing Performance Study, giving and receiving criticism each rank among the top ten most stressful situations in the workplace.[2] To drill down into why that is, let's explore six of the more (and less) obvious stress factors associated with engaging in a criticism exchange.

—1—
Criticism Is Rooted in Negativity

At its core, criticism will never be positive and was never intended to be. The giver of criticism is pointing out some degree of negativity regarding someone's behavior, mannerisms, or actions by using words and expressions of nonapproval, and it's that negativity that produces stress.

—2—
Workplace Criticism Comes at Unexpected Times and Triggers Real or Imagined Consequences

Interestingly, when we participate in sports, the arts, or any kind of activity that involves a paid coach or instructor, most of us expect criticism. When paid instructors don't point out something we are doing wrong, it's not surprising that we question whether we are getting our money's worth.

As it relates to the workplace, earlier research that Bright Learning Enterprises conducted with Simmons Market Research Bureau found that workers really do expect to be criticized by their bosses.[3] What makes workplace criticism so stressful is the nagging worry that involves wondering if any consequences are associated with the unexpected criticism.

During a lesson with an instructor, criticism is most often confined to the classroom or workshop, the intent behind it is understood as helpful, and students consider it as guidance leading to the development of skills. However, in the workplace, an employee may have no idea that something she said or did might be subjected to another's judgment. Often, the intent behind a criticism in the workplace is unclear. Closely associated with the unclear intent—and a major underlying stress-producer—are the imagined or real consequences associated with being criticized by, for instance, a boss or supervisor. In the workplace, employees can't always be sure the criticism is a "coaching moment"; it might instead be some form of chastisement and therefore something to worry about in the future. Furthermore, nagging questions can come up and linger for months as employees worry about whether those critiques will become strikes against them during their next performance review. In settings where we are paying for lessons or being coached, we have no particular reason to get stressed about potential consequences behind criticisms that happen to come our way.

—3—
Criticism Can Destroy Relationships and Cause Hurt Feelings

The devastating and destructive consequences of poorly handled criticism come as no surprise. When growing up, many of us recited the phrase "Sticks and stones may break my bones but names will never hurt me." Since criticism knows no age limits, there's an adult version: "Sticks and stones may break my bones but words can break my heart." Adults are all aware of criticism's potentially destructive nature. The stress related to criticism comes when the receivers aren't sure whether the intent is to help, hurt, rattle their self-confidence, or set them up for a fall.

Back in the 1980s, a study conducted by Rensselaer Polytechnic Institute captured the attention of professionals in the fields of communication, emotional intelligence, and human interaction. The researchers found that one bad criticism exchange could destroy a working relationship. It takes a long time to build trust and respect, but these feelings can easily be torn down by an inappropriate use of criticism.[4] Recognizing the potential carnage that criticism can cause, it's no wonder that past experiences lead many managers to avoid saying anything at all. They might go as far as creating excuses, such as "I just can't say anything. After all, my people are working so hard and they aren't getting big bonuses or raises—and, well, it just wouldn't be worth the hassle it might cause." Perhaps what's really going on is that they don't want to jeopardize their relationship with an employee in the event their criticism might create a hassle that results in lowered motivation levels.

—4—
Unlike Praise, a Criticism Exchange
Can Become Nasty

Unlike a compliment or piece of praise, a poorly handled criticism exchange can quickly become nasty. When praising someone, we rarely worry about how the person will respond. However, when we engage in a criticism exchange, the conversation can start out smoothly, much like performing a dance, and then suddenly become clumsy as the rhythmic dance turns into a tangle of bruised and battered toes—all because the receiver suddenly takes offense at what is said. Indeed, criticism can become a sticky wicket in a relationship the instant it is given. And it can happen anywhere, anytime, and to anyone, no matter whether it is a coach, instructor, boss, fellow worker, staff member, mate, close friend, or family member.

Let's consider a manager who must tell an employee that her clothing is inappropriate for the office setting. The employee interprets the statement as an insult and judges her supervisor to be insensitive. Besides being resistant, for the next few days the employee is abrupt and does her best to have little contact with her boss. In another example, a peer innocently uses an unfortunate selection of words and tone of voice when honestly commenting about a team member's proposed idea. The critical comment soon results in a gnarly argument as both sides dig in their heels and begin to engage in personal attacks.

Not uncommonly, when receivers react defensively to criticism, it is their interpretation of the giver's intention that comes into play. Combined with the history of the relationship and how the criticism is delivered, it can turn into a pitched conflict where the giver is left owning the result. A recent article in the *Wall Street Journal* reported that 25 percent of a manager's time deals with conflict.[5] What we don't know from the study is what percentage of those interactions is the result of poorly handled criticism, but it's likely that it's a lot.

—5—
Embedded in the Delivery of Criticism Is the Perceived Need to Change

Unlike praise, criticism usually implies the need to make a change in attitude, the way we think, or the way we behave. Just having to deal with change by itself can be stress producing. Additional stress is created when the change isn't to our liking. I once worked with a veteran manager who used a command-and-control style of leadership in an organization where that style had fallen out of favor. HR and top management pressured the manager to be more inclusive and collaborative and to generally behave more in harmony with the times. To the manager, that approach was certain to be ineffective because it was "too soft." Very likely, the stress of change was part of the manager's response. Any leader is likely to experience doubt and discomfort when he has successfully performed a task a certain way and is now told that it's not the way to do it anymore. Criticism, such as in this example—where change is required more than suggested—can result in both hurt and resentment. And, if handled poorly, such criticism can seriously hamper one's performance.

—6—
Poor Delivery and a Nonreceptive Receiver Both Play a Role

The vast majority of us are poorly trained in both giving and receiving criticism, and it's the lack of effective skills that creates additional stress when we are engaged in an exchange. It's not unusual for supervisors and managers to receive training in how to deliver performance reviews. Whether that training should go farther and comprehensively cover the topic of criticism (from the perspective of both givers and receivers) is up for debate. Nevertheless, performance reviews tend to be formal and based on a set schedule. They are certainly not the only occasions when skillfully delivered (and received) criticism in the workplace needs to be attended to. Just as important are the countless interactions that bosses, coworkers, and teammates have with one another throughout the workday. It is in those moments that we see just how much the proper training is lacking.

There are all too few resources available for the average person who wants to develop skills in the very important area of effective communication with regard to relationship interaction. Books and training guides usually treat criticism in a way that is very prescriptive, requiring some canned approach that makes the givers sound rehearsed and insincere, while the receivers seem like pliable and receptive mannequins. These books and guides completely miss the point that, for it to be accepted and acted upon, criticism has to be sincere and its purpose needs to be genuinely perceived to be of help to someone. It is a skill that, when managed properly, can change relationships and people's lives for the better.

THE TOP TEN COMMON MISTAKES MADE BY GIVERS OF CRITICISM

Always remember that for criticism to be accepted, it needs to be delivered effectively and it must come across as helpful. And therein lies the skill! The effort to develop this skill will have lifetime value for you and those with whom you deal.

COMMON GIVER MISTAKE #1:
Givers Call It as They See It

Those giving criticism who speak before they think often refer to themselves as the type of people who "call it as they see it." They typically overlook where and when they choose to give criticism. Their approach is based on an emotional reaction with little thought given to the consequences. These are the "Quick Draw" givers. Those who are in the habit of quickly calling it are often vulnerable to embarrassment when they are shown to be wrong, misinformed, or inappropriate.

Quick Draw givers underestimate the emotional power of criticism, especially when receivers (and those in hearing distance) fail to see the helpful purpose or value in what's been said. Quick Draw givers often gain the reputation of being too reactionary or critical, and they are rarely considered to be good bosses, good teachers, or good coaches. They alienate more than they motivate. They overlook the fact that once they open their mouth, the control shifts to the receiver, who decides how to interpret what's been said. The way criticism is perceived might be likened to someone retelling what she believes to be a funny story only to have the other person view what's said as horrifying or shocking.

So avoid being a Quick Draw giver. Recognize that your control lies in the proper preparation. It involves considering such things as what to criticize, how to express it, when, where, and by whom. It requires developing the habit of thinking before you speak. This is good advice for all of us. Before opening your mouth, stop long enough to think, "What's my exact purpose, and what do I want from the person [the receiver]?" If your purpose is to humiliate or embarrass, then zip your lips. That's not a productive use of criticism, and your statement should not be voiced. Careful preparation is the most important thing you can do before giving criticism to others, be it at work, at home, or among friends.

COACHING TIP #3:

Avoid the Consequences of Bad Criticism

Warning! The consequences of poorly delivered criticism can be serious, can permanently destroy relationships, and can result in the loss of a job, a marriage, a friend, or the respect of entire teams.

Think about a relationship that soured or abruptly ended. Ask yourself if poor communication played a part in the deterioration of the relationship. Then, delve even further (like peeling the layers off an onion) and ask if criticism played a part.

In many cases, you'll find that poorly delivered criticism has a part to play in the destruction of relationships.

COMMON GIVER MISTAKE #2:

The Criticism Is Delivered According to Where, When, and What's Comfortable for the Giver

Feeling uncomfortable when giving criticism is natural, but many people think that having an uncomfortable feeling inhibits the success of their delivery. As a result, with or without their awareness, they do things to regain a sense of comfort. Generally, they deliver criticism according to how they prefer to receive it. These givers are more about "me" than they are about taking into consideration the preferences and needs of the person receiving the criticism. These "More About Me" givers, in their desire to be comfortable, also believe in taking to the limits such biblical platitudes as "Do unto others as you would have them do unto you" or "Treat others the way you want to be treated." More About Me givers are likely to subscribe to such ridiculous prescriptive advice as "Start positive, move negative, and then end with a positive." Pathetically, it's a simple formula that keeps them comfortable and does nothing for receivers.

You don't want to fall into the habit of being a More About Me giver. For starters, your goal is not to be comfortable when giving criticism; rather, the goal is to be effective. Delivering helpful criticism is a skill, much like learning how to give an effective sales pitch. Just as salespeople need to be sensitive to the quirks and perceptions of those they are selling to, so too do you need to be sensitive to getting buy-in from the receiver. You need to step outside yourself and factor in what you understand to be the receiver's preferences and needs. As discussed in Chapter 3, there should never be any guessing about how best to approach someone you work closely with or—all the more so—someone who is significant in your life.

That canned idea of starting positive, moving negative, and ending with the positive should never be relied upon as an effective formula for interaction. The real problem with this technique is that after all is said and done, many people remember only the negative. The problem can also work in the reverse, where receivers hear none of the criticism because they are too busy basking in the positive. In addition, if the receivers did hear the criticism, they frequently undervalue its significance as it compares to the praise. Furthermore, when receivers become accustomed to this often-used, unfounded, and risky tactic, they fail to acknowledge any of the positive because they are waiting for the sharp ax of criticism to fall. This positive-negative-positive sequence is often referred to as the "cookie approach" or the "sandwich approach," and its very nature implies that an individual is not unique and that all people can be expected to respond positively to this formula. If you use this approach on a consistent basis, you will soon have kids, employees, and anyone else who endures your style of criticism comparing experiences, and you'll wind up the brunt of their derision! So remember, it's most effective to treat others the way *they* want or need to be treated.

COMMON GIVER MISTAKE #3:
The Message Has a Personalized Rather Than Instructive Tone

Givers of criticism who make this mistake are called "Hey You" givers because they keep personalizing the criticism by referring to "you" throughout the delivery. These Hey You givers fail to recognize that many receivers have their guard up when being criticized because they tend to think any criticism is a personal attack. To protect themselves, these receivers are watchful for certain words or phrases such as "You should have known," "I pay you too much money," "You are experienced enough," or "I'm disappointed in you." When receivers hear these words or sense that the criticism is personal, imaginary alarms go off. Then, they quickly shift their focus from the situation at hand to the broad question of their competence. The underlying message and tone from Hey You givers is blame, and the implied message picked up by receivers is "You're guilty." As a result, receivers suspect that the Hey You givers may not have their best interest in mind. They may even conclude that Hey You givers would rather catch people doing things wrong than set them up for success.

When delivering criticism, you want to depersonalize your message by staying in the third person or the passive voice. For example, say "This report is late" rather than "You are giving me this report late." You could say, "To engage the audience more, the idea could have been presented by talking first about benefits," which is more effective than "You did not present your idea very well because you didn't talk about benefits, and as a result you failed to engage your audience." Delivering your message in the third person or the passive voice keeps the conversation focused on the issue at hand. It's not about "you" and it's not about "me versus you," which is what happens when the message is personalized.

What we are talking about here is not to be confused with another common practice that some of us have been taught—"Criticize the behavior, not the person"—which helps to depersonalize the message. You don't say, "You have a bad attitude. When a new idea comes up, you are quick to take a negative stance." Rather, focus on the actions in general, and in doing so, put it in less personal terms. You can say, "When a new idea is presented, it's best not to take a negative stance." Notice that the latter approach is instructional in tone rather than accusatory. Now, your comments have a universal application and could apply to anyone in any organization.

Focusing on the behavior also helps the people receiving the criticism better understand what they are doing wrong. A word of caution when using this "focus on the behavior and not the person" rule: Skilled givers of criticism understand "gray areas" between what is and is not personal. If the criticism had to do with a male employee's hairstyle or the way a female manager dresses, it's personal. You can't implement this rule in these cases. You'll learn more about addressing these sensitive situations recognizing the "boundary limits of criticism" in Chapter 3, which deals with creating an atmosphere of acceptance.

COMMON GIVER MISTAKE #4:
Givers Leave the Person Receiving the Criticism Guessing About How to Correct a Situation

Givers who make the mistake of letting receivers guess what actions they need to take may come across as being very polite when pointing out what someone is doing wrong. Being polite and well intentioned is important, but it won't accomplish much if there is no specificity. Take the person who says, "You need to be more organized," "You need to take more initiative," or "You need to keep me better informed." Besides noting the personal focus of the accusation, receivers typically walk away from such an exchange not totally sure of what they need to do to correct the situation. They may make several unsuccessful attempts to satisfy the giver by trying to correct the situation. Instead of feeling good about the changes they are attempting to make, receivers typically become confused or frustrated because they start to think that no matter what they do, they can never quite satisfy the person. The giver keeps leaving them guessing, and in time, he becomes known as a "Guessing Game" giver. Gaining that kind of reputation is not a good thing!

In order for criticism to be helpful, it's important to devote time to discussing specifically what you want from the other person. Let's say that you (the giver) have been caught by surprise on several occasions when meeting with senior management. You tell your employee (the receiver) that you want her to keep you better informed so you are not at a loss during meetings. That's a start, but the message still leaves the receiver guessing. Do you want her to stop by your office periodically throughout the day to give you quick updates? Do you want a written weekly or monthly report? You need to clarify how and when you want your employee to keep you informed, and you need to discuss what you want included in the report. This exact situation occurred in a U.S. government military garment factory with a plant manager and his five direct reports. The boss had his team in a stew because although each team member provided monthly reports, the boss kept complaining that he wasn't getting what he needed to stay informed. He never seemed to be satisfied. Finally, with the help of an outside consultant, a meeting was arranged where the five direct reports asked the boss what he wanted. They were all caught by surprise, as was the consultant, when the major thing the boss said was that he didn't like the way the reports were formatted. All that frustration and wasted time and energy could have been avoided if the boss had from the start discussed up front what he wanted and how he wanted it.

COMMON GIVER MISTAKE #5:
The Giver Generalizes the Criticism, Leaving the Receiver Confused

We come now to criticism givers who resemble Guessing Game givers because they lay out a general problem but fail to fill in the holes with any specific examples, leaving receivers confused about what is being done wrong. These are the "Donut Hole" givers who base their criticism on nonspecific or questionable assertions, leaving the receiver to feel resentful or unfairly criticized. For instance, take the supervisor who tells her direct report, "An employee came into my office yesterday complaining about you. And from what I can see, it all adds up to the fact that you intimidate others." Or a president tells his direct report, "I need you to be nice" when addressing the topic of executive presence. In each case, the Donut Hole giver fails to provide the necessary specifics in order to help receivers understand what they are doing wrong. If these givers add something like "I wasn't there," or "I don't know, but I thought I should bring this to your attention," it sounds weak and only increases receivers' frustrations.

If you don't have all the information and you want receivers to know you have their best interest in mind, it's important for you to go to the source, if possible, to obtain the specifics. It's a matter of taking the time, or more accurately making the time, because when you do, there's a greater chance that the criticism will be accepted. Most importantly, it's making the effort to convey quality information that the receiver can work with and learn from. As a bonus, it helps foster trust and respect.

In addition, offering specific instances or examples to illustrate what the receiver may be doing adds credibility to the message, especially when the receiver has no awareness that he may be doing whatever the criticism is based on. For instance, it could be using a lot of "ahs" or "ums" when speaking or talking too loudly or too fast. A criticism directed at a habit or repeatedly bothersome behavior (such as not looking at the person he is talking to or using too many "uhs" when he speaks) can be totally out of his realm of awareness. All the more reason why pointing these habits out needs to be done in a clear and specific manner.

COMMON GIVER MISTAKE #6:
The Giver Overlooks the Empathy Factor

"Who Cares?" givers have a lot in common with Quick Draw, More About Me, and Hey You givers because they show little concern for the receiver. Who Cares? givers are either in a hurry and pressed for time or so intent on correcting the situation that they fail to recognize emotions that are being experienced by the receiver.

Here are two quick examples. An employee is given an "urgent report" to complete by his boss late in the day on Friday. The boss is panicking about the report because she needs to deliver it on Monday to top executives who are coming in from Corporate. After the employee works slavishly all weekend to finish the report, he proudly presents it to his boss early on Monday morning only to have her immediately spot a few errors in the financial section. Without even looking up, she says, "You didn't include the forecast numbers and now it distorts the final revenue picture." Or take this second example, where a boss has been out all day and upon returning learns about a customer complaint. Without questioning what kind of day the customer service manager has had, the boss approaches the manager and blurts out, "We have a problem with yet another customer that you and your people need to handle."

Most likely, the issues in these two examples will get resolved, but at what cost to the relationship between the boss and the employee? What's unknown is the extent of the destruction that's been left behind as the receivers repeatedly replay in their minds the insensitivity of their bosses. As author Maya Angelou's well-known quote reminds us, "People will forget what you said, people will forget what you did, but people will never forget how you made them feel." All the boss had to do in each situation was be more sensitive to the employee's circumstances. In the first example, she should say, "I know this was a rush and that you put personal time into this report, but we do need to get the financials corrected." Even though issues may appear urgent at first glance, you still can factor in the individuals and their unique situations and consider where they are coming from emotionally.

In the second example given here, the boss could have asked the customer service manager what kind of day he had before bringing up the customer complaint. If the customer service manager had a great day, all the boss had to do was say, "Well, this is not meant to put a damper on your day, but I just learned about a customer complaint that you and your people need to handle." What if the customer service manager had a terrible day? Well, if the boss determined that the situation was urgent, then she might open the conversation by saying, "When it rains, it pours. I just learned about a customer who's very upset—so this is something you and your team need to handle." If it's not urgent and the situation could wait until the next morning, she might decide to tell the manager to go home and have a restful night because in the morning he needs to address a customer issue.

COMMON GIVER MISTAKE #7:

The Giver Easily Loses Focus During the Exchange

"Where Were We?" givers are tripped up by receivers who are skillful at shifting the point of the criticism and moving it to another topic. Take a look at this receiver's response, for example, when her supervisor criticizes her (his top performer) for being repeatedly ten to fifteen minutes late for weekly staff meetings: "Why are you always picking on me? I am the only person on the team who met all of last year's goals." The boss responds by saying, "I'm not always picking on you. What makes you say that?" and then, within that instant, the topic of the conversation passes to the command of the employee regarding how often she is "picked on" by the supervisor. Or what about the receiver who says to his peer, "Well, you may not like how I handled this email exchange, but you don't even respond to email in a timely manner." His peer replies, "That's not true! What makes you say that?" Another tough one for Where Were We? givers is when the receiver responds to a criticism by saying, "I hate it when you use that tone of voice with me," and the giver takes the bait and responds, "What about my tone of voice?" In each example, the Where Were We? giver is off to Mars when he wanted to stay on planet Earth.

To approach these sly receivers, it's important for you to determine your purpose ahead of time. Some people have found it helpful to put the purpose of the discussion in writing or print; when it veers off, all they have to do is point to the topic on the monitor or paper. Visibly displaying the topic of discussion encourages everyone to take responsibility for staying on point. Others have found it helpful to establish expectations up front. Prior to engaging in the conversation, the giver might try saying something along the lines of: "In order for us to have a productive conversation, let's agree to stay on topic. As other topics come up, let's jot them down so that we can make a point to address them later. If we allow ourselves to jump from one subject to another, given the limited amount of time we have, we will end up accomplishing very little. Can we agree to this?"

By simply agreeing to stay on topic, you can save time, prevent confusion, and maintain working relationships. It also helps to keep the giver in command of the purpose of the conversation. If no expectations have been established, such as in the stop-picking-on-me matter, givers can still keep on topic by saying, "We can talk about whether I am picking on you later, but right now, let's address the need to be on time for meetings." Keeping the conversation focused helps to ensure a productive exchange where, in the end, something is resolved.

COMMON GIVER MISTAKE #8:
The Giver Fails to Point Out Any Benefits

This mistake is made by givers who assume that the benefit of the suggested behavior change is somehow implicit in the criticism. These givers are referred to as "Just Do It" givers.

To illustrate this point, let's use the example of a successful rising star manager whose name is Ted. Ted was transferred from the East Coast office of a Southwest-based company to turn around a team whose performance was considered by upper management as woefully substandard. Besides having interpersonal relationship issues, members on the team had fallen way behind on their technological skills.

Ted came in like a bull to stir things up, which, unfortunately, he did so rather too successfully! You see, in his haste to point out issues and start them on the way to resolution, Ted made the team members extremely upset by his abrasive, confrontational style, and they ran to Ted's boss, Sam, to complain. Sam recognized the urgency of the situation, and as a "Just Do It Giver, " she rushed over to Ted, telling him he was too confrontational. Ted resisted the criticism from Sam because he believed that shaking up the team was exactly what he was brought in to do.

All the confusion that resulted between Sam and Ted in the days that followed could have been avoided if only Sam's message had placed the criticism in proper context so Ted could understand what Sam was saying more clearly. Achieving a better outcome when delivering the criticism could have been done easily and simply by linking the criticism to their shared team goals. Sam could have said something like: "Let's step back a minute and remind ourselves of what it is you are trying to achieve with this team. The goal is to get the team to work together effectively and to encourage them to share their technical expertise with one another in an effort to sharpen their skills. Using a confrontational approach with this team is not effective. Instead, it has had an opposite effect. There is a contentious situation possibly brewing where it is a 'you against them' situation. That's not where we want to be. We can't afford to make matters worse. I'd be glad to discuss other approaches with you. Perhaps I could be of greatest help if I more clearly explained to you our culture."

The thing to focus on from this scene is the fact that Ted would have understood the intent behind Sam's criticism more clearly from the outset if Sam had linked the criticism to the broader goal. Sam needed to explain more clearly the reason Ted needed to change his behavior. All too often, people do not link the broader goals involved with criticism they give to others.

Now lets briefly examine a typical off-the-job example that readily applies to the workplace. A father criticizes his son for coming home late without letting him know in advance. The benefit or value of the criticism is unknown. Under such conditions, the son is left to his own imagination, and when that happens, it's not out of the question for him to come up with faulty conclusions. For instance, the son might conclude that his father doesn't trust him or is just being "too controlling." Instead of letting the son come up with such faulty conclusions, the father should explain that when the son doesn't call, the father worries that something could be wrong. Also, the father's own plans for the evening become disrupted. It's the father's position that the matter is more about respect and not distrust. Pointing out the value helps the son understand his father's point of view, and he is therefore more apt to accept the criticism.

This scenario is no different from what occurs in the workplace when a boss criticizes her direct report for not keeping her informed of his whereabouts. Instead of having the direct report think that his boss is a control freak or doesn't trust him (which might typically be the case), the direct report would have a different reaction if the value was linked to the criticism. To make things clearer, all the boss had to say was, "When I'm in a meeting with my boss or other executives and they raise a particular topic, it's embarrassing to have to admit that I'm in the dark. It's almost as if they have one up on me. When I'm kept informed of what's happening in your department, it helps tremendously." When the value behind the criticism is clearly explained, the actions that need to be taken become meaningful, and the person being criticized can readily understand that the intent of the criticism is to be helpful.

The point being made with all these examples is that in order to be made acceptable, criticism needs to be delivered in a way that appears helpful to receivers. In fact, any other reason for giving criticism should be considered invalid.

COMMON GIVER MISTAKE #9:
No Consideration Is Given to Varying the Intensity of the Criticism

"The Sky Is Falling" givers are readily discovered in the workplace and quickly characterized as prophets of doom. With these people, all criticisms are treated equally, regardless of the weight of their importance or urgency. Very often, The Sky Is Falling givers accompany their criticism with exaggerations and use words to create impact. "Your report's a disaster," they might say when spotting a single mistake. "No one will want to buy this product after listening to that horrible sales pitch," they might say after hearing your sales presentation. You can identify The Sky Is Falling givers at home because they often blurt out things like "The house is a mess" or "The kitchen is a wreck." Rarely are specifics offered. When such exaggerated criticisms are delivered, it's as if these givers are intending to shock those within hearing distance. With time, those on the receiving end quickly dismiss the urgency and severity of the error. As a result, The Sky Is Falling givers quickly lose credibility. It's important to remember that mistakes and errors vary in importance. Not all criticisms should be delivered with the same intensity.

To help you think about the severity of the criticism and the need to vary it, let me share a memorable interview I had years ago with a mother whose teenage son had suffered a serious sports injury. She decided to spend the first night of his hospital stay with him in his hospital room. She remembered lying awake in the silence of that room as her son slept. She found herself pondering the future and thinking about what she would do differently in raising her son. The realization that kept repeating itself was how she regularly criticized him. Delving further, she became aware that she never altered the intensity of her criticisms. When I asked her to elaborate, she explained: "I never considered weighing the importance I placed on any one criticism. For instance, I would criticize my son as harshly for leaving his shirttail out before heading off to school as I would for not completing a report, which was far more important."

When you stop to think about a criticism, you want to consider the importance of the mistake you're pointing out and tailor your message accordingly. This adjustment will make the receiver more apt to view the criticism as helpful in its intent. Again, it's the receiver who's in control after the message has been communicated! When people are criticized harshly for something they see as trivial or relatively unimportant, you can expect them to say something along the lines of "So, what's the real problem here?"—because there probably is one.

COMMON GIVER MISTAKE #10:
The Giver's Timing Is Bad

Too often, criticism is delayed, and the longer it's delayed, the more stressful and challenging it is for the giver to bring up the topic. These "Procrastinating" givers often operate with the belief that if they wait long enough, the situation will correct itself or the problem will somehow magically disappear. But what happens if the problem doesn't go away? Actually, most such problems persist. As Dr. J. R. Larson, a psychologist at the University of Illinois, describes, "Most problems in an employee's performance are not sudden; they develop slowly over time."[6] Therefore, when Procrastinating givers are reluctant to say anything, what's happening underneath the surface is the personal buildup of frustration and stress. It's like sweeping dirt under a rug. You can't see it, but it's there. Ultimately, so much dirt accumulates that someone walking over the rug eventually trips. That's what happens to Procrastinating givers. When they figuratively trip, it is equivalent to blowing up and saying things that are far more damaging than if the issues had been dealt with early on in the situation. Too often, sparks fly back and forth because receivers are caught off guard.

Because nothing has been said before, receivers are falsely led to believe that everything has been satisfactory, at least to this point. However, when the criticism is finally blurted out, the receivers are confused and may start asking all kinds of questions as they quickly move into a defensive position. At that point, it's not uncommon for receivers to reject the criticism altogether. When this happens, conversations can become ugly. Unfortunately, Procrastinating givers in the end run the risk of tearing down whatever trust has been built in the relationship. Perhaps the most common example of trust being shattered occurs when an employee learns for the first time during a performance review what the boss views unfavorably.

There really is no upside in being a Procrastinating giver. However, while you don't want to postpone delivering criticism, you also don't want to go to the extreme and point out every mistake as soon as it occurs, as Quick Draw givers (discussed previously) are apt to do. Knowing when to point out a mistake and bring it to the attention of the individual is part of the skill associated with giving criticism. You need to judge whether the situation is a onetime event or whether it's something that, if not addressed, most likely will continue. Being late for a meeting or adding up some figures incorrectly, for instance, may be just a fluke. You can make a mental note of the situation and say nothing. On the other hand, let's say you and a colleague are meeting with your boss's boss, who you know happens to be a real stickler for proper grammar. During your three-way conversation, your colleague says, "between he and I." You think that perhaps you should say something about this after the meeting, but you decide that it would be too late then because the damage would be long-lasting and the impression irretrievable. So you decide to interrupt your colleague immediately during the conversation, saying, "There you go—I know you mean 'him and me.' Sorry for interrupting." Later, you explain to your colleague how the interruption saved his butt! Hopefully, that explanation conveys that you're interested in his well-being and are being helpful. But it's not a guarantee!

THE TOP EIGHT COMMON MISTAKES MADE BY RECEIVERS OF CRITICISM

Just as giving effective criticism is a skill, being an effective receiver also requires skill. All of this takes patience, practice, and the ability to think practically.

Becoming a skilled receiver starts with understanding that in a criticism exchange, the real control of the outcome belongs to the receiver. It is the receiver who decides whether a criticism that comes his way is valid or not. One way to think about criticism is to view it as the last game of the last set of a tennis match where the score is 40-40. The server might seem to have the advantage at this point, just as a giver who is delivering criticism does at the time the criticism is given. In the tennis match, once the server serves and smokes the ball over the net, he transfers control of the game to his opponent, who can now decide to rip it back, lob it, spin it, or wait to see if it lands inbounds or out. If he takes proper control and makes a skillful return, the crowd hears the words "advantage receiver." Just as in a tennis match, the receiver of criticism is on the side of the net where a cool head and a good sense of judgment are prerequisites for staying in the game. It's not about winning or losing, though. Criticism, when handled properly and effectively by both givers and receivers, is about benefiting from what others say by being candid and open and ultimately learning how to get better.

To get you started on your journey toward becoming a more skilled receiver, let's explore where many receivers go wrong. Keep in mind that benefiting as the receiver goes beyond simply knowing that the receiver is in control. It also requires knowing how to put that control to use even if you are interacting with an unskilled giver—and there are plenty of them out there!

You will learn all you need to know about the skill involved in dealing with criticism as a receiver in Chapters 5 and 6 of this book. For now, let's explore some areas where receivers fail to exercise their control.

COMMON RECEIVER MISTAKE #1:
Making the Giver Feel Uncomfortable

"I'm Being Attacked" receivers overlook the fact that most givers have been poorly trained in giving criticism. Instead of trying to work with givers, I'm Being Attacked receivers instantly become defensive, fire off questions, and challenge the givers in order to protect themselves. These receivers fail to see that making givers uncomfortable is likely to bring out the worst in them. They also fail to recognize that in the end, they run the risk of not obtaining what could be very valuable information. Think about it: What givers would want to get into a hassle every time they offered what they think is helpful feedback? Over time, these givers will shut down and put the need to say something at the bottom of their action list.

You may be surprised to hear that when you are on the receiving end of criticism, it is your job to make the giver feel comfortable. After reading this the first time, you may think it is an error. Let me explain how it's not and what's behind this valuable insight.

Imagine yourself as a manager or project leader who has an opportunity to form your own team. Whom would you want on your team if you had just two employees to choose from? The first candidate is technically competent and has a reputation for being easy to work with. This reputation comes from his willingness to admit mistakes and be open to suggestions. Compare this employee to your second candidate, who is technically a superstar but becomes defensive and argumentative when approached about errors she has made. She has been known to justify her mistakes by blaming others. When it comes to selecting your team members, if you are like most skilled leaders, you may select the second employee if the project requires superior technical expertise. You would, in essence, need to bite the bullet! However, if technical expertise is not a specific requirement for the project, then you may be inclined to select the first employee. After all, there is enough stress to go around, and who wants to select someone who is difficult to work with on a regular basis? Though others in your department might think it strange that you did not select the person with the stronger expertise, your awareness of the importance of temperament in your overall work environment will in time prove you wise.

Being known as a receptive receiver—and certainly not as an I'm Being Attacked receiver—will help you to get assigned to challenging and visible projects. Being receptive in this way plays a key role in your advancement and that of just about everyone else in your organization. In the short run, if you make givers comfortable, you gain valuable information you need to help you reach the outcomes you desire. Don't be misled by the fact that you rarely hear from management that people didn't get promoted or assigned to a challenging project because they are not receptive to criticism or feedback. In many organizations—where even the mention of the word "criticism" is a cultural "no-no"—you can bet that having a reputation for being a nonargumentative receiver is an important characteristic to have going for you!

COMMON RECEIVER MISTAKE #2:
Failing to Listen and View What's Said
as *Information*

When you are on the receiving end of criticism, how you listen is one area where you have control. There's nothing wrong with listening to argue and judge. If you are deciding where to send your child to school, for instance, and are listening to what the counselor or school official is saying, it's natural to judge whether or not you like what's being said.

However, when you are the receiver of criticism—whether at work, with friends, or at home—you want to make a point of listening to understand and not being an "Argumentative" receiver. Why? For starters, remember that most givers haven't read this book and most likely are poorly skilled in their delivery of criticism. Next, and just as important, when you listen in an argumentative or judgmental way, you are automatically creating a right/wrong, agree/disagree, win/ lose condition. Putting a lot of emphasis on weighing whether you agree or disagree with the criticism before taking the time to fully hear and consider what is being said can spark a defensive response. Not a good way to promote a productive exchange!

Listening to understand and viewing what's said as "information" is beneficial because it helps to neutralize the message. From there, you want to ask yourself, "What is this person trying to tell me?" Just taking the time to ask and answer this question may be all that's needed to keep you from firing back and saying something you later regret. Instead, you'll end up asking more questions in order to better understand what the unskilled giver is trying to say. Remember, as in a boxing match, there are many rounds during which you interact with your boss, coworkers, friends, and family members. You don't have to fire back with a deadly blow. In the big picture, you don't want to "win the battle and lose the war." So avoid being an Argumentative receiver and listen to understand instead of being quick to judge.

COMMON RECEIVER MISTAKE #3:
Failing to Stop, Think, and Investigate Before Reacting

Never, ever be the kind of receiver who is unassuming and takes whatever givers dish out as truth. Remember that as the receiver, you have the control. Always take full advantage of that control and inspect what criticisms are coming your way. It's important that you sort out good, helpful criticism from criticism that is truly meant to be damaging and hurtful. After all, in the workplace, not everyone has your best interest in mind. Sometimes criticism is meant to throw you off balance and rattle your self-confidence. You need to consider the intent behind the criticism and inspect whether the criticism is accurate. You also need to assess if the poor delivery of criticism is mainly due to the giver's lack of skill.

When taking control, you don't want to be a "Quick Responder" receiver. These receivers have a lot in common with Argumentative receivers because they too listen to argue and judge. As soon as they get wind that they may be wrong, they are ready with a quick response to defend themselves. The only trouble is that they fail to note the difference between facts and opinions because not all facts communicated are meant as criticism. Take, for example, the boss who says to a team leader, "The project to date is $2,000 over budget." Before the boss can take a breath and continue, the Quick Responder receiver is ready and fires back, "It's not possible to stay within the budget given all the reworks we have had to do. Our suppliers are not delivering what we need, and it's causing us a lot of overtime." If Quick Responders aren't careful, bosses can come back and say, "Hey, slow down. Don't get so defensive. I'm merely pointing this out so you know where we are financially. I know you've run into trouble with our suppliers. I'm just trying to have a conversation with you, but it's a little difficult when you get so defensive right away." Now the boss is thinking to himself, "I have two issues. The first is the budget, and the second is a team lead who is difficult to talk to because he gets immediately defensive."

As the receiver, you are in control of determining whether what's said is a criticism or not. You want to be skilled at listening for facts versus opinions or perceptions. Rather than immediately make the leap and view the facts as implied criticisms, possibly embarrassing yourself, you may want to use your control to ask the giver for help in interpreting what has been said.

Granted, this may be hard to do when you are dealing with someone who doesn't have your best interest in mind. Even so, you have the control and it's up to you to use it. Don't give the person that much authority to shake you up.

COMMON RECEIVER MISTAKE #4:
Jumping to Quick Conclusions

A frequent mistake receivers make is trying to remedy a criticism right away by doing what they believe needs to be done. The trouble occurs when these "Instant Fix-It" receivers are unsuccessful after making several attempts. Frustration and disappointment set in, and eventually they reach a point where they say, "No matter what I do, I can never satisfy my boss, coworkers, mate, family members, or friends." Take, for example, the boss who says, "You need to take more initiative and be a problem solver." The Instant Fix-It receiver takes matters into his own hands and starts making decisions on his own. When the boss talks about a particular problem, the Instant Fix-It receiver sets himself into motion and takes the boss's discussion as a command to fix the problem. Then, when the boss learns that the Instant Fix-It receiver has invested time and energy to address the problem, the boss gets upset because the issue raised was only in a discussion phase. This opens the door for the boss to find out about other things that the receiver is doing without the boss's knowledge, and the boss criticizes him for going too far. The Instant Fix-It receiver then finds himself in a tizzy over what to do next.

You never need to get caught up in a guessing game. Don't be fooled into thinking that the corrective action is embedded in the criticism, especially when dealing with perception-related criticisms.

What you need to do is find out what the desired action is—from the giver's perspective, not your own. Whether the criticism concerns your need to take more initiative at work, listen better at home, or act more professional, you want to learn from the giver what she wants you to do differently. Whatever you do, don't guess. *Investigate!*

COMMON RECEIVER MISTAKE #5:
Focusing More on the "How" Than "What" Is Being Said

Don't get caught up with the "how." Focus instead on the "what." Some "Be Nice" receivers are easily thrown off and tune out if the giver's tone of voice, choice of words, volume of speech, hand gestures, or looks are not to their liking. They are known for telling givers, "There's that look again," "Don't talk to me like that," "I don't like the way you are approaching me," or "What do you mean I should have. . . . " Too often, these receivers can't hear the criticism because they are in the habit of listening more for "how" the criticism is being delivered rather than "what" is being said.

By now, you realize that how you listen is in your control. If you allow yourself to tune out "what" the giver is saying, you will be at a disadvantage when hearing criticism from a crude, unskilled giver. Why? Because beyond the giver's potentially crude delivery may be some valuable insights that you'll miss because you've tuned him out. So like a laser, cut through the distractions and get past "how" the message is delivered and beyond the words used. Instead, zoom in on what's being said or, more accurately, what's "trying to be conveyed." Because you have the control, you can always come back later when emotions are calmer and clear the air by discussing your turn-ons and turnoffs related to how criticism is delivered.

COACHING TIP #4:

How to Know If You Are Listening to Argue and Judge

There are a number of self-reflective clues to look for to indicate whether you are on your way to adopting the dangerous habit of listening to argue and judge.

One helpful clue requires paying attention to what you are saying. If you hear yourself starting a sentence with "No, that's not what happened," "You're wrong," "That's not correct," or "I disagree with you," then there's a strong likelihood that you are listening to argue and judge.

Another clue requires listening to your thoughts while you are listening to others. If you find yourself mentally arguing with what they are saying as they are saying it, *stop!* That is the first sign that you are on your way to arguing. Stay open until all the evidence is in.

Finally, if you use your gut and feel things, then your clue is when a feeling comes over you that says, "I'm going to prove this person wrong—even if I don't believe in everything I'm saying." This feeling is about digging your heels into the sand to win your point. Listening to argue and judge is not the best way to engage in a productive criticism exchange because most givers are not eloquent in their delivery. It's better to listen to understand, which involves asking yourself repeatedly: "What is the person trying to say?"

COMMON RECEIVER MISTAKE #6:
Blaming Others or Circumstances and Failing to Admit Mistakes

In order to be trusted and respected by others—whether it's your boss, peers, coworkers, friends, or family members—it's important to admit your mistakes. That doesn't mean waiting until you're questioned. It means volunteering information up front when you've erred. Admitting mistakes sends a message to others that you are approachable. It also demonstrates that you are willing to be honest with yourself as well as with others. Avoiding the "Innocent Until Proven Guilty" receiver's attitude goes a long way in building trust and respect. At times, it's very hard to admit a mistake, especially when you take pride in doing quality work and getting results. Keep in mind that in the long run, others will forget the mistake, but they will bear in mind how you handled the mistake. Successes and mistakes come and go, but your character describes who you are, which builds your reputation within the organization—and that sticks!

COMMON RECEIVER MISTAKE #7:
Personalizing Criticism Before Being Sure It Was Meant to Be Personal

The tendency to take a critical comment from a boss, coworker, family member, or friend to heart is natural. "Take It to Heart" receivers are not alone. Survey findings from workers in the Northeast revealed that being on the receiving end of criticism is the second greatest producer of stress in the workplace.[7] It can create an emotional earthquake and cause confidence levels to shake or even crumble.

As you will learn in Chapter 6, people interpret "personalizing criticism" differently. The most common interpretation of personalizing criticism is "having an immediate emotional reaction that impairs thinking and the ability to engage in a meaningful exchange." All too often, we tend to immediately interpret criticism as being about ourselves. We let it rattle our self-confidence. Very few of us learn to develop a thick skin and not let critical comments made by others pierce through like a knife through Jell-O. Participants in the Strategies for Enhancing Performance Study who were introduced to de-emotionalizing skills found vast improvements in their ability to stay in control and remain objective.[8] These de-emotionalizing skills—which are all about avoiding the tendency to personalize criticism—are introduced in Chapter 6.

To get you started with the proper mind-set, here are some valuable perspectives to consider about criticism in the workplace. For starters, recognize that being criticized in the workplace is no different from being handed unexpected assignments or having to face tight deadlines. It comes with the territory, and it's only business.

Rather than try to avoid criticism in the workplace, recognize that it's a given and learn how to benefit as the receiver and avoid personalizing it. Avoid holding on to the perspective that when you are criticized, you're "bad" or a "failure." Rather, view criticism as an opportunity to do things better in order to achieve specific goals. Even if the criticism is directed at you personally, it still doesn't mean you are perceived as a failure or a bad person. Your image is not destroyed. Helpful criticism is frequently delivered to assist you in going from "good" to "even better." It's valuable to keep in mind that many bosses look at an employee's potential and try to tap into it by creating challenges, which may or may not eventually involve some criticism along the way.

A final valuable perspective to hold on to is that the criticisms you receive are frequently related to your role and are not directed at you personally. An executive director, for instance, was accused by her direct report, who was also her friend outside work, of monitoring her too closely. Yet the executive director was simply fulfilling her role as a leader who recognized that "you only get what you inspect, not what you expect." Following up and holding people accountable are what bosses need to do. Perhaps the direct report had changed the rules because she allowed their friendship to color and reshape their working relationship. Whatever the situation, it's important to remember that your role often is a breeding ground for criticism. Think of those who work in payroll, collections, the print shop, or customer service. The criticisms launched aren't directed at them; instead, they are associated with the role they are being asked to perform. At times, it may seem as if fulfilling your role is similar to playing forward during an ice hockey game. Just as the forward is trying to score goals and will likely get bumped and pushed along the way, you too may experience critical comments as you proceed to do your job and fulfill your role. It comes with the turf!

COMMON RECEIVER MISTAKE #8:
Allowing Oneself to Become Victimized by Givers Who Don't Know What They Want

"I'm a Victim" receivers work for bosses who don't seem to know what they want. Consequently, when work is presented, these bosses typically do not like what they see. When criticism comes from such bosses, receivers feel they have been dealt with unfairly because they thought they delivered exactly what the boss requested. It's not uncommon for these receivers to feel victimized by the circumstances of not knowing. While these situations don't lend themselves to easy, prescriptive-like solutions, there are specific steps you can take to deal with these types of givers.

Start by remembering to utilize your control by coming up with your own solutions. That doesn't mean you should go out and solve the problem on your own. Doing that can result in wasting a lot of time and energy and can lead to even more frustration. That's operating as an Instant Fix-It receiver. Avoid getting caught in that pitfall. Instead, develop a solution and pass it by your boss to make sure you are directing your energies productively. For the boss who isn't clear about what he wants, be prepared to go through several rounds before you're finished and have your marching orders and a boss who is pleased. Remember, each time you are criticized, it's getting these bosses closer to what they want.

Matt, for instance, worked for a boss who always changed her mind. She would tell Matt to do something, and when he brought the completed assignment to her, she would criticize what he had done. As she was pointing out what he did wrong, Matt would think to himself that he had done exactly what she had asked. To avoid feeling victimized, Matt decided to take control by summarizing at the end of a meeting what he was planning to do, being sure to describe the task's end result. Providing his boss with that kind of detailed description helped determine if he had heard her correctly and if he was working on the right thing. Sometimes he sent the summary to her the next day in an email. Another tactic he used was to break the task into various parts. Each time he finished a part, he would pass it by her. Using this approach helped to prevent a whole lot of rework. To avoid taking the criticism personally, he realized that this was the way he needed to deal with his boss on the completion of tasks. It wasn't about him. After all, she had rated Matt very highly on his last two performance reviews. He lowered his frustration level by realizing that his job wasn't to change his boss. Rather, it was to work with her. Also, his job wasn't to judge her. Instead, his job was to understand her. In the final analysis, Matt may not always like working with a boss who operates this way, but at least he's not a victim.

BECOME A BETTER COMMUNICATOR: REMEMBER THE DOS AND DON'TS OF CRITICISM

We've just discussed some of the common mistakes made by givers and the receivers of their criticisms. You should leave this chapter with an appreciation that for both givers and receivers, what you say, how you say it, when you say it, and how you take it are all skills that require thought before action in most cases. In the chapters that follow, you'll learn how to refine your skills even more so you can communicate more effectively with others and engage in productive, candid conversations. What you are doing in the big picture is engaging in a different kind of accountability. Most of us are familiar with the importance of being accountable for what we do. You are now taking accountability for what you say.

Perhaps the lack of skill in the handling of criticism has contributed to the bad reputation criticism has in business and industry and helped to promote the trend of a kinder, gentler philosophy where leaders and coworkers are concerned about hurting each other's feelings. This trend is also occurring in education, where teachers shy away from being too demanding and harsh. It seems as if in both settings, this prevailing philosophy has gained traction and embraces Abraham Lincoln's wisdom that "a drop of honey catches more flies than a gallon of gall."[9] But in education, at least, this soft approach is now being challenged. K. Anders Ericsson, Michael J. Prietula, and

Edward T. Cokely, in their article "The Making of an Expert," convincingly argue that top performers—in fields ranging from violin performance to surgery to computer programming to chess—"deliberately picked unsentimental coaches who would challenge them and drive them to higher levels of performance." A key part of their message is that "expertise requires coaches who are capable of giving constructive, even painful feedback."[10] Like teachers in education, perhaps it's time for managers and leaders in business to wake up and do what works to get consistent results.

As we will learn in Chapter 3, developing receptivity to criticism begins with establishing clear expectations.

Quick Review for Easy Recall

The following are among the reasons criticism in the workplace is so stressful:

► You are not sure when someone is judging you and you say something, there are implied consequences associated with the criticism, and it's not clear whether the intent is to be helpful or hurtful.

► Poorly delivered criticism by an unskilled giver is hard to swallow. On the other hand, a nonreceptive receiver can make the person giving the criticism extremely uncomfortable.

The top ten mistakes made by givers of criticism are being:

1. Quick Draw givers, who "just call it like they see it"

2. More About Me givers, who deliver criticism according to how they prefer to receive it

3. Hey You givers, who personalize the criticism

4. Guessing Game givers, who let receivers guess what actions they need to take

5. Donut Hole givers, who lay out the problem but don't provide specific examples

6. Who Cares? givers, who show little concern for the receiver and are more focused on correcting the situation at hand

7. Where Were We? givers, who easily lose their focus

8. Just Do It givers, who assume the benefit of the suggested behavior change is somehow implicit in the criticism

9. The Sky Is Falling givers, who give all criticism equal weight regardless of importance or urgency

10. Procrastinating givers, who just wait, hoping the problem will magically disappear

The top eight mistakes made by receivers of criticism are:

1. Making the giver feel uncomfortable

2. Failing to listen and view what's said as information

3. Failing to stop, think, and investigate before reacting

4. Jumping to quick conclusions

5. Focusing more on the "how" than "what" is being said

6. Blaming others or circumstances and failing to admit mistakes

7. Personalizing criticism before being sure it was meant to be personal

8. Allowing oneself to become victimized by givers who don't know what they want

CHAPTER 3

Creating an Atmosphere of Acceptance

Establish Clear Relationship Expectations

> *The motive behind criticism often determines its validity. Those who care criticize where necessary. Those who envy criticize the moment they think that they have found a weak spot.*[1]
>
> —CRISS JAMI

Once again, Tim's technical lead, Jerry, has let him down. When Tim checked with Jerry earlier in the week, Jerry told Tim that he would have what he needed by Friday morning. It's now Friday at 3 p.m., the technical plan is nowhere in sight, and neither is Jerry. Tim has heard nothing from him, which further adds to his frustration. On top of everything that's on Tim's plate, he now has to contend with this. Tim is ready to explode because this isn't the first time Jerry has let him down. He doesn't want a big showdown over the matter. All he wants is for Jerry to deliver what he promises and to at least communicate the status of the project.

Typically, when Tim had tried to address the subject of Jerry's failure to deliver as promised, Jerry would nod his head as if in agreement, but then he would continue to go off in other directions and miss crucial deadlines. Nothing ever seemed to change. But what if Tim had a way to engage Jerry in an honest exchange where both openly shared their thoughts, as opposed to having their discussions end in disappointments?

Like all of us, Tim needs to know how to create an atmosphere within relationships where a potential for conflict gets minimized and where criticism, when needed, has a greater potential for being accepted and acted upon without question or debate. By the time you are through with this chapter, you will have the insights needed to make criticism work when it is needed. You will understand how to create an atmosphere of acceptance among employees and coworkers so that they understand and are willing to deliver and receive criticism and view it as helpful rather than negative or hurtful.

That atmosphere of acceptance of criticism is made up of four simple yet powerful ingredients:

1. Mutual levels of trust and respect need to exist.

2. Goals and what's personally important need to be mutually understood.

3. There needs to be a clear understanding of how best to approach others with criticism.

4. There must be a realistic understanding of the boundaries that define your relationships.

THE FIRST KEY INGREDIENT OF RELATIONSHIPS:
Mutual Levels of Trust and Respect

Why engage in the topic of trust? Because our society is so diverse today that the values that were once common among us and that linked us together may no longer necessarily be assumed. For this reason, to save time in the process, and most importantly to avoid misunderstandings, it's imperative today to engage in conversations in order to learn about each other's likes, dislikes, and sensitivities that may in fact have cultural underpinnings.

Here are a few subtle indicators that trust levels may be question-able:

► You hear someone is "surprised" that you said something nice about her.

► Someone acts fidgety or nervous when you find yourself alone with him (for instance, on an elevator).

► While engaged in a conversation, someone who typically makes eye contact instead looks everywhere but at your eyes.

► Someone often responds to you by saying, "Do you mean it?" or "Are you telling me the truth?"

► Someone you work with seems shy about voicing her opinion in your presence.

People who speak or act in such ways are not quite ready to take criticism from you even though you may be their boss or instructor.

Both trust and respect are essential aspects of a climate that allows acceptance of criticism. Where there is a high degree of trust in a relationship, we generally assume positive intent as the motive behind any criticism that is given. We rarely question the motive or second-guess givers of criticism when we trust and respect them. When we trust someone, we pay attention and listen—even if it hurts.

Because of this understanding of positive intent, we allow coaches, teachers, guidance counselors, and therapists to criticize us, usually without question or argument. We believe, in most cases, that their motive is to help. In addition, we respect these people as qualified to offer us help even though they can be highly critical of our behavior. We trust that they'll be honest with us and let us know when we do or say things that run counter to our mutual interests. However, with some relationships, especially those at work, we often don't know one another well enough to have a solidly established trust relationship. We don't know whether those we interact with are confident that we are clearly operating with one another's interests and benefits in mind. So when it comes to people we don't know very well, we need to initiate steps designed to let each other understand what is in our mutual interests and what we expect from one another. We need to carefully establish *matched expectations* that will provide a basis for allowing us to best proceed in our cooperative dealings.

When expectations are established and agreed upon up front, the need for guessing is eliminated and there are fewer chances that criticism resulting from misunderstandings will be required.

When I was a diver preparing for the Olympic trials, I had a nationally renowned coach. Early on in our relationship, he talked about how we would work together. He explained, "As long as I'm yelling at you and being hard on you, it's because I believe in you. When I stop yelling, that's when you'd better start to worry. Is that okay with you?" I agreed, and the two of us enjoyed a successful working relationship for years. During practice events, spectators would watch in various degrees of horror as my coach cursed and criticized me after a dive. Nevertheless, I would chuckle inside because I knew that he believed in me and was trying to push me to do more than I felt capable of doing. His positive intent was that one day I could make it to the Olympics, and he would be there by my side.

When parties follow through and uphold their established agreements, trust and respect are fostered and the foundation of the relationship is strengthened. Think of the people you work with who are "easy" and "low maintenance." Most likely, you enjoy working with them because goals are understood and generally achieved. You don't have to second-guess what's expected of one another, and a sense of openness exists in your dealings and conversations. You can usually count on them to come through and deliver whatever was promised or agreed upon. All this equally applies to our relationships at home and with friends.

When expectations are mutually understood and upheld, trust and respect are enhanced, and there becomes less of a need to use criticism. On occasions when criticism is needed, it will have a greater likelihood of being perceived as having a positive intent behind it. In turn, that sense of positive intent cushions the negativity of criticism and promotes agreement rather than conflict. Now and then it's valuable to have a conversation about trust and what goes into the building of trust among people you interact with regularly. Regardless of your rank or position in your company, engaging in a conversation about trust will likely only begin with your deciding to broach the subject.

COACHING TIP #5:

Ideas for Opening Up a Conversation About Trust

▶ Email a friend or coworker a blog or article on trust commenting about what you thought was interesting or how it reflects your views.

▶ Bring up the topic by referring to a recent movie or TV program that you both watched.

▶ During a casual conversation, ask a question about trust, for example, "Do you grant people trust up front, or do you believe trust is built over time?"

▶ Simply make a statement to start a dialogue, for example, "You are someone whom I feel I can always rely on. And I want you to know that you can rely on me to stick to our agreements. Okay?"

THE SECOND KEY INGREDIENT OF RELATIONSHIPS:
Mutual Understanding of Goals and What's Personally Important

A clear understanding of goals and objectives is vital to make criticism work. It is the foundation upon which criticism acceptance is built. When criticism is given and goals are understood, the negativity of criticism can be minimized and criticism becomes viewed as helpful.

Establishing goals is common in the workplace. Take, for example, the following scene, which is an actual situation that occurred recently between a young married couple, Mary and Mike. They both share the desire to be supportive of each other in their lives and careers. In personal relationships with loved ones and friends, setting goals is often a less formal process, where wishes and intentions are not always clear and mutually understood. It upsets Mary that Mike frequently works late during the week and on weekends and, consequently, is not spending enough quality time with the family. Mike can't understand why Mary doesn't realize that he has a demanding boss and, if he wants to keep his job, he simply has to put in all of these hours. Mary recognizes that Mike has a big job with lots of responsibilities and a boss who expects loyalty to the company. But she thinks he goes too far, and his lack of involvement with the family puts too much of a burden on her. The dialogue they get into almost sounds like a song that gets played on a regular basis. The lyrics go something like this:

Mary: Here you go again! Late as usual. All you think about is your work. We don't matter in your life. I can never count on you!

Mike: Mary, I'm sorry! What am I supposed to do? My boss sends me an urgent email right before I'm about to leave telling me to handle an issue with an angry customer who is worth a lot of money. And you know how tough things have been at work!

Mary: It's the same old story. If it's not an angry customer, it's a problem in operations or IT. It's as if you carry the weight of the company on your shoulders. Why doesn't your boss handle some of these issues? He makes the big bucks. They don't pay you enough for everything you do at the company. They own you. You care more about the company than you do for us!

Mike: That's not true, Mary, and you know it.

The lyrics usually drop off at this point as both partners have delivered their lines, leaving nothing really resolved—only to be replayed at another time.

When you don't know or share how best to approach the achievement of goals, you have fertile ground for the eventual outbreak of the kind of criticism that can lead to arguments and the type of harsh exchanges that Mary and Mike experience. Once again, expectations need to be clarified and mutually agreed upon.

Equally as valuable is knowing what's important to others. This distinction is important because those we interact with may not always have well-articulated goals. Generally speaking, people who interact with one another on a frequent basis, whether on the job or off the job, have good instincts about what's important to one another. Often, we learn about the importance placed on things via casual conversations. With friends, we may learn that a secret is meant to stay a secret when confidential information is shared. We may find out the importance placed on returning emails in a timely manner or the priority placed on having open and candid conversations. In the workplace, we may uncover what's important to an individual during a job interview or a performance review discussion. During those discussions, you might hear, "If I'm doing anything wrong, please let me know right away. That way, I won't have to waste my time working on something that I know is not to your liking or isn't important to you." For the person saying something like that, receiving feedback on an ongoing and timely basis is important. Or we may hear, "What I'm looking for in this job is to be challenged and to have an opportunity to learn." Many bosses have heard employees say things along the lines of: "I went to school to study X technology or to learn about Y application, and what disappoints me about this job is that I get no opportunity to use any of those skills."

Other employees may be interested in issues of compensation. Likewise, some may place great importance on being praised when they did a good job, showed diligence about being on time, or were attentive to details.

Let's return to Mike and Mary. Certainly, both know that it is important for Mike to keep his job. Mary feels it is equally important that Mike spends time with family and that weekends are special. If they don't work out a balance of their differences regarding their expectations, they run the risk of engaging in a series of criticism exchanges where as soon as one episode is over, another is bound to occur down the road.

Whether at home, at work, or among friends, our assumptions of others' goals and what is important to them need to be investigated and confirmed. Take a moment and think about people who are important in your life, asking yourself if you truly know what's important to them. A note of caution: What was important yesterday may not be today. Also ask if you know how best to be supportive of one another. In the workplace, a valuable question to ask employees after assigning a task is, "How can I best support you?" This is a great question to raise, especially given today's attempts to empower others. Oftentimes, when a boss seems too earnest while checking in on how a project is progressing, employees interpret the earnestness as lack of trust.

Are you sure you know what other people's goals are? Do they know yours? Having these discussions and getting on the same page eliminates a lot of tension and arguments that could lead to criticism exchanges. Just asking questions of others that relate to their goals, likes, and dislikes can be a giant step in creating trust in relationships, opening the door to the acceptance of helpful criticism and communication that builds rather than destroys.

It's common to assume that because we love someone or have worked with him for a long period of time, we know how best to approach him with criticism. Not so! Even with loved ones and long-time associates, we need to talk about these things occasionally to make sure that our assumptions remain on target.

THE THIRD KEY INGREDIENT OF RELATIONSHIPS:
A Clear Understanding of How Best to Approach Others with Criticism

We each have a preference for how people talk to us. Some people want to be spoken to honestly and directly, while others need to have things sugarcoated and delivered more carefully. Delivering criticism can be like approaching a wild animal. And depending on the type of animal you are dealing with, you are going to approach the individual with varying styles. Is your receiver a bear or a bunny? You need to know before you approach the person with any kind of criticism.

While all of us know that criticism will come our way every so often, we also know that it is the way it's delivered that makes it work or not. The real questions are: Do others know what, when, and how we are willing to accept criticism? Do we know what others' preferences are that will make them more inclined to accept criticism from us?

To eliminate the guesswork and minimize the stress, why not learn how best to approach each other with criticism right up front? So, how do you do that? *Ask them directly!* We ask our loved ones what they like to eat, what clothes they like to wear, and what types of books or movies they enjoy. Likewise, in the workplace, it's not unusual for bosses to explore employees' career aspirations or what type of work they like to do. Since we know criticism is inescapable, why not ask their preference for how we should best approach them so they don't take it the wrong way?

What typically happens is that we deliver criticism without giving much thought about how it is dished out. Take, for example, James, who provides support services to financial advisers at a major bank in New York City. After a recent reorganization, he wound up reporting to Shari, a successful manager whose advancement up the corporate ladder has been very rapid. Shari demands a lot from her people, and she gets them to rise to the occasion. She has a reputation for "saying it like it is." During their weekly one-on-one meeting, Shari gets right to the point and talks to James in a harsh, don't-challenge-me tone:

Shari: James, why waste your time working on setting up this management meeting? I pay you too much for you to handle logistical items. Get your people to do this.

(James is taken aback by her forcefulness.)

James: In the past, I've been the one who . . .

Shari: I don't care what you've done in the past. You work for me now, and you have too much to offer this company to waste your time on such frivolous activities.

By the next day, James had delegated the planning of the meeting to his team, as Shari had requested. Because Shari got the results she was looking for, she never gave the conversation another thought. Unbeknownst to Shari, though, James has been replaying their exchange over and over again in his mind. Each time, he concludes that he doesn't like being interrupted. He finds it rude and disrespectful. He also was turned off by her harsh tone and the fact that she wasn't even interested in what he had to say. These aspects of Shari's delivery of criticism, unless brought out in the open, will eat at James and over time will negatively affect their relationship. All the while, Shari will be totally in the dark about the whole thing—but she doesn't have to be. All Shari needs to do to strengthen the trust relationship with James is ask him his sincere thoughts about their exchange and tell him it is okay to be honest about it.

If the receiver appears receptive, we—like Shari—make a mental note and try the same approach a second and third time before drawing some conclusions. If the receiver does not respond favorably, then we try something different. Using this trial-and-error method of learning requires good instincts, a number of experiences, and good mental note taking. Guessing wrong, however, can cause long-lasting resentment that undermines what could otherwise be a healthy relationship. In the workplace, the trial-and-error approach seems to be quite popular, as is delivering the criticism in accordance with how you prefer being approached—which is equally risky. (There is more about that when we actually zoom in on how to deliver helpful criticism in Chapter 4.) For now, what's important is that those we interact with, both at work and at home, all have a pretty good idea of what turns them off and what makes them more receptive to criticism. What's key is to ask.

COACHING TIP #6:

What to Do if You Feel Awkward Approaching a Coworker About Engaging in a Conversation About Criticism

Often, what's associated with feeling awkward is not being comfortable getting started. Here are some of the best ways to get started:

- ► Open up the subject during a casual, nonpressured time. Go for coffee or casually stop by the person's cubicle or office.

- ► Set the stage and start the conversation by saying, "A bunch of us were talking about our favorite bosses. So, tell me about a favorite boss you have worked with." An effective follow-up question to ask is: "How did your boss approach you when you made a mistake or failed to deliver on something?"

- ► Use the effective starter approach of saying, "We have some major projects ahead of us that we need to work on together, and I wanted to discuss your thoughts about how we can best work together." Sometime during the conversation ask, "How can I best approach you about a mistake that's been made and still keep the conversation productive?"

> ► Be sure to be a good listener. Your focus is to understand what the other person says, not to judge it.

THE FOURTH KEY INGREDIENT OF RELATIONSHIPS:
A Realistic Understanding of the Boundaries That Define Your Relationships

Have you ever been caught by surprise when criticizing someone because he felt you were off-limits? Perhaps it was when you criticized an employee for not pursuing an advanced degree in school or for not attending corporate-sponsored events after work. In each case, the response from the employee went something like: "That's my business" or "Who are you to tell me?"

What better example of off-limits criticism than the recent statement made by Connie Mariano, the former physician to the president of the United States, about the weight of New Jersey's governor, Chris Christie. During a CNN interview, she said that she "worries about this man dying in office." Christie gained the attention of the media and viewers when he shot back a rejection of the criticism, saying, "A doctor in Arizona who's never met me, never examined me, never reviewed my history, or medical records, knows nothing about my family history, could make a diagnosis from 2,400 miles away. She must be a genius." Just to demonstrate the power of criticism, Christie's twelve-year-old son heard Mariano's claims and felt concerned enough to ask his dad if he was going to die.[2] In Christie's mind, the doctor's criticism moved beyond that fine line of criticism, where it is rejected on the basis that it is viewed as an insult!

All of us started learning about social boundaries in childhood. They were our first guidelines for how to get along. They came from our mother, grandmother, father, grandfather, uncles, aunts, and sometimes older brothers and sisters. You may recall having been told to "never talk back to an adult." Some of us were told to "never criticize the teacher." Others may have been told, "If you don't have something nice to say, don't say anything at all." As we were growing up, we created our own boundaries. When we were young, a parent was clearly justified in criticizing us for our messy bedroom or telling us which friends to socialize with and which to stay away from. However, as we entered our teenage years and began to learn about our "right to privacy," the bedroom suddenly became our sanctuary, and criticism about its condition was an offense to what was now considered our domain: "It's my room and my mess, and I'll live with it. Leave me alone!" Similarly, when our parents or other adult figures told us which of our friends they accepted and which they didn't accept, we often felt that we could justifiably and rightfully ignore them—at least according to the terms of our newfound independence. We might have considered their pleas, but it was another story for us to adhere to their requests and demands.

Now, as adults, we still live with boundaries, and there are lots of them. Try asking your current mate or spouse about details of former love affairs, and see where that conversation goes. In the workplace, bosses try to create an environment of give-and-take by saying, "You can be open and tell me what's on your mind." Really? The research my company did in collaboration with Simmons Market Research Bureau showed that when in doubt as to whether or not to criticize the boss—don't![3]

Generally, employees assume that criticism directly related to work is within allowable bounds, provided it comes from a qualified source. One's boss or a respected teammate may be a qualified source, and therefore considered inbounds for certain kinds of criticism. However, some other coworker who has a terrible reputation may not be perceived as qualified and is therefore viewed as out of bounds in giving us any type of criticism. Criticism in the workplace related to more personal things may be considered out of bounds regardless of who is giving it. For example, can one's personal taste in clothing become a legitimate matter of criticism in the workplace? It probably can if it comes from the boss and if workplace policies include a dress code by which all employees are expected to abide. However, if no dress code has been officially established, an employee criticized for her choice of clothing could be justified in rejecting such criticism. While boundaries must be established, clarified, and understood before criticism is given, most of the relationships we have with our friends, coworkers, and family members don't have neat, tidy boundaries regarding giving and receiving criticism. To reach a level of understanding about the boundaries within which criticism is allowable, we need to get to know one another fairly well. But just getting to know one another doesn't automatically equate to building a receptive atmosphere. We might think we know our family members well enough to criticize anything, but try criticizing grandma's apple pie, and then prepare for flying plates!

Of course, boundary issues can come about and catch the other party by surprise. Consider this example of a relationship where otherwise compatible coworkers are working on a project together. They may be spending hours together in meetings and communicating by email or phone. They have thoroughly discussed how best to perform various tasks in order to complete the project. The professional goals of the two may seem rather clear, but the boundaries may not be. If one of them doesn't complete a task on time and is berated by the other, the giver of the criticism could easily find himself hearing such bitter complaints as: "Who are you to say anything to me? I don't report to you. My schedule got too busy. It just so happens that I had to do something for my boss, so I couldn't get this task done. I'll get it to you as soon as I can." Or consider the case of friends gathering at someone's home for dinner, and one of them brings up politics. The noise level quickly rises as friends rant and rave and criticize each other as if the words exchanged were a tennis ball in a doubles match, only to have everyone caught by surprise when the host blurts out that talking about politics at her home is not accepted!

While our national joint Simmons Market Research Bureau and Bright Learning Enterprises survey on criticism has shown that employees expect to be criticized by their boss, it doesn't show that conversations involving criticism routinely result in productive outcomes free of conflict. Take, for instance, Martha, who has worked for her boss, Larry, for more than six years. During her last performance review, Martha was rated as "exceeds expectations," which is the highest rating she could achieve. Receiving such an outstanding performance review is the norm for Martha because she works very long hours, is competent, and consistently performs above expectations. All the good feelings from what her boss said quickly faded when Larry casually said at the end of their meeting that she had "better start coming to work a little bit earlier" now that her office was "located next door to the big boss." For the next two weeks, Martha fretted about what Larry had said to her. She had never been late to work as far as she could remember. She felt that it was unfair and, yes, out of bounds for her to be expected to come to work earlier than others in her department. If she had only asked Larry for clarification, she would have discovered that he was just trying to be helpful since he knew that the "big boss" admired managers who arrived at work earlier than the employees. A word of advice: Boundaries need to be reviewed now and then from the standpoint of both givers and receivers.

COACHING TIP #7:

Always Clarify Mutual Expectations with Friends, Relations, and Coworkers

Have you established mutual expectations in key relationships? Check yourself by considering the following:

► Build a list of the people at work as well as off the job who are of key importance to you.

► Ask yourself whether you can accurately answer the following questions about each of these important people:

▶ Are you sure you know what [name]'s goals are?

▶ Are you sure you know what's important to [name]?

▶ Are you sure you know how best to approach [name] with criticism so he/she doesn't take it the wrong way and will recognize the positive intent?

▶ Are you sure you know how best to support [name] in his/her efforts?

▶ Are you sure you know what equates to building trust in a relationship with [name]?

If you have answered "yes" to all of the questions above, then you are well on your way to creating mutual expectations, and you will rarely feel like you are walking on eggshells when interacting with these people.

However, if you answered "no" to any of these questions, then you have some homework to do! For those questions where you answered "no," your next step is to turn that "no" into a "yes" by taking initiative to ask the person directly. After all, these are the people who are important in your life. To open up the conversation, you could say, "I was reading a book that asked some insightful questions about relationships, and it occurred to me when thinking about you that I may have assumed certain things about you that may not be accurate. You know what happens when you assume something. So I'd like to ask you . . ." Keep in mind that you need to set the stage by explaining why you are bringing up the topic. Otherwise, the other party will question where you are coming from and will be confused about your motives.

Your timing of when to engage in a conversation like this is also important. If at work, consider stopping by someone's office or work area and asking if he has a few minutes. Ideal times are when you are going out for a cup of coffee or lunch. It's best to keep it casual. Another great time at work to engage in this type of exchange is during the performance review. When it comes to family members and friends, casually have these conversations frequently and preferably during a neutral time as opposed to when in the heat of the moment.

When you are taking a "no" and turning it into a "yes," you are helping to shape and build an atmosphere of acceptance for future productive exchanges and are simultaneously continuing to further strengthen the relationship. In essence, you are addressing *unspokens*—the culprit for misunderstandings in relationships.

DISCOVERY EXCHANGES: ESTABLISHING THE "MATCHED RELATIONSHIP EXPECTATION PACKAGE"

Unfortunately, mere awareness of the four ingredients of relationships is not enough. It's putting them to work that counts.

Asking the people you care about and those who are important in your life the questions outlined in Coaching Tip #7 yields a wealth of knowledge and insight. In the workplace, when managers and employees have worked together for a period of time, there's a hesitancy to ask these questions because people think they should know these things by now, and bringing up the topic may seem awkward and out of place. However, when these same managers and employees have taken the lead and engaged in conversations that center on how best to be open with one another or how best to keep each other informed, they are pleasantly surprised by the other person's receptivity to have these discussions. When I have asked bosses directly about whether it is necessary to have these types of conversations, they typically have an expression on their face that says, "Why are you questioning the need?" Then they immediately say, "How else are we to know how best to work together if we don't talk about these things?"

I call these conversations "discovery exchanges." For all their value, it's often difficult to initiate them. Here's a valuable insight: When investing time to engage in these discovery exchanges, don't be surprised if the other party complains that the conversation is overdue. An employee might say to his boss, "I can't believe we've worked together for three years and you didn't know that about me!" Don't let the conversation get off course. Its purpose is to gain an accurate awareness and, from there, to establish a mutual understanding where both parties agree to follow through and uphold their established agreements.

Engaging in these two-way conversations is extremely valuable and a great time-saver. Because time is at such a premium today, in the workplace we often rely on various behavioral inventories such as Myers-Briggs, LIFO, and Profile XT to learn how best to relate to and work with one another. These inventories help describe people's behaviors and personality types. Some people are described as extroverts or driven types who are more action oriented, while others are called introverts or analytical types and are more thought and data driven. Applying these generalizations helps when you are first getting to know someone, but it can be detrimental to rely solely on such generalizations. Humans are more complex, and besides, they can change.

We also try to gain insights about others by factoring in generational differences in an effort to ensure quality communication. As one manager in his fifties confessed, he was "surrounded by Millennials in their late twenties" and it was "a struggle." He would bark out orders and point out errors in rapid-fire fashion, only to find that his team began to lose enthusiasm for accomplishing tasks correctly and in a timely manner. He quickly changed his approach to assigning tasks and invested more one-on-one time with employees. It wasn't long before he saw a noticeable difference in their enthusiasm for their work and a positive difference in their attitude.

Relationships are dynamic and need to be nourished. It's up to you to start this process no matter what relationship is involved. Take a moment to be certain you are thinking candidly about all of the people who play a key role in your life, and consider what it takes to start, strengthen, and build relationships. When considering how best to engage in conversations about trust, support, what's important to individuals, and how best to approach one another with criticism, it becomes apparent to all that you have sincere intentions for helping to shape and define relationships with those at work and at home.

Whether you seek out clues from the use of behavioral instruments or generational descriptors or decide to engage in two-way exchanges with those you care about and need to work with, the objective is to establish what I call a Matched Relationship Expectation Package. This is when you have a clear understanding of what's expected from others and what they can expect from you. When there's a mutual understanding that's agreed and acted upon, then there can be true receptivity to criticism.

Let's return to Mike and Mary and highlight the Matched Relationship Expectation Package they established. During their discussion, Mike helped Mary appreciate that his perfectionist tendencies, combined with his boss's analytical style that gets embroiled in details, causes Mike to invest extra time when preparing reports and presentations. As a result, both agreed that on the weekend, Mike is to get up early to do his work before the rest of the family gets moving. That way, he can enjoy family activities during the rest of the day. On Sunday nights, again by mutual agreement, he could check his emails while dinner is being prepared. Since Mary and Mike worked out this understanding, things have been much better and the tension between them has dissipated.

THE IMPORTANCE OF UNDERSTANDING AND CLARIFYING UNSPOKENS

So, why can't all parties in relationships work things out like Mike and Mary? They can. However, relationships often run into difficulty and become a breeding ground for conflict when people fail to recognize and accurately interpret *unspoken expectations*. Unspoken expectations are those kind of expectations that are not communicated verbally or in writing. They are not overtly expressed like spoken expectations. Despite the fact that nothing is communicated verbally or in writing, these expectations nevertheless still operate. Sometimes unspokens are referred to as "implicit messages" or "unwritten rules." When expectations are not clearly communicated or remain unspoken, relationships can become strained when those involved try to figure out what the other person wants or how best to work with that person. This results in creating a need for guessing, which can be dangerous. If you guess incorrectly, you could get into big trouble! To spot unspokens, start by being a good listener. You need to pay close attention to what certain words mean or probe what may be unclear in an effort to pick up on what the person is thinking but not expressing. You need to clarify your conclusions or assumptions by letting others know what they are and letting people validate them or dismiss them as inaccurate. When it comes to what we expect of others and what they expect of us, it becomes all important that we are not guessing and that we are sure.

All relationships operate with unspokens. Let's revisit Tim and Jerry, whom you met at the beginning of the chapter. Rather than get upset with Jerry, as Tim has done in the past, Tim should approach Jerry at a time when neither of them is facing the pressures of having to meet a deadline. During a casual conversation, Tim should explore what's important to Jerry. Since it's a two-way exchange, Tim can emphasize how he places importance on keeping agreements and operating with no surprises. From there, the conversation could clarify an important unspoken that Jerry has two commitments when working on a project. One commitment is delivering the technical plan at the quality level expected, and the other is meeting the deadline.

Let's listen in to get a clearer understanding of the exchange.

Jerry: I understand that meeting deadlines is important, as is doing quality work. As I mentioned to you, I place importance on completing projects on time. It's just that when I'm working, I get so many interruptions. People are constantly asking me questions.

Tim: I realize that your expertise is in high demand.

(It suddenly hits Tim: The unspoken here is that while Jerry said meeting deadlines is important, what may be more important to him is satisfying requests from others. Jerry has a hard time saying "no.")

Tim: Jerry, do you have a hard time turning down those requests?

Jerry: Absolutely! Sometimes it only takes a few minutes to address their issues, and other times it takes a couple of hours. The only trouble is after I work on a few of their requests, my day is practically gone, and I don't have time to work on these longer-term projects that you've asked me to work on.

(Tim and Jerry work out a plan for handling everyday requests. From there, the discussion moves to how upset Tim gets when he hears nothing from Jerry.)

Tim: As I mentioned at the beginning of our conversation, I don't like surprises and I don't like the fact that when we have these blowups, nothing changes. You knew the deadline was Friday at noon. How could you let that deadline come and go and not get back to me to tell me you were going to be late?

Jerry: I don't know. I apologize. I guess I get so wrapped up in what I'm doing that I lose track of time.

(It occurs to Tim that Jerry is not fighting him. His intentions are good. Tim has a hunch. It's an unspoken that just occurred to him when hearing Jerry's comments. But before he brings it up, he decides to check with Jerry about whether Tim does an effective job supporting Jerry after assigning a major project.)

Tim: Is there anything I can do differently to support you better when assigning these projects?

Jerry: No. I think everything's fine.

Tim: By any chance, when you work do you have a clock visible in your office? *(This is Tim's unspoken.)*

Jerry: No. I use my cell phone to check the time.

Tim: When you work, do you periodically look at the time to see how you are doing in relation to a deadline?

Jerry: I guess not. I become so obsessed I don't look at it.

That was all Tim needed for the two of them to work out a plan for making sure that Jerry pays more attention to the due dates. Tim also knew that he and Jerry needed to have a further conversation to work around time-related issues and keeping each other informed.

What's being emphasized here is the importance of picking up on unspokens in a conversation. When you do, you tap into the heart of an issue and are much better positioned to come up with a solution that has some potential for success. When unspokens are spotted and accurately interpreted, you work with quality information.

A classic unspoken that many receivers fail to consider is that when they are being criticized, the people doing the criticizing are interested in them. At least they took the time to say something even though you may not like how they delivered the criticism! Step back for a moment and think about those people whom you really don't like or care about. If they are doing something wrong, would you say something to them, or would you more likely say nothing at all? How many times have we heard people say, "I wouldn't give that person the time of day." Here's another important unspoken that I learned from my research. When receivers are being criticized, the following thoughts often go through their mind: "I have blown it. Will he ever see me in the same light again?" "She will never trust me again," "He's lost faith in me," or "I've ruined my chances for any kind of promotion." In each case, people are interpreting criticism as a sign of permanent rejection and are making a giant leap in logic requiring some quick clarification! As a side note, what I found to be very helpful is to say to the receiver, "This is only a criticism, not annihilation! I still believe in you."

COACHING TIP #8:

Be Clear About Creating Mutual Expectations

People who criticize without discussing solutions are doing little more than simply chatting.

Here's a quick workplace example where two workers are "chatting" about respect and one of their coworkers:

> **John:** I was really taken aback by how Bill never called us to let us know he would be late for our meeting today. This is the second time he's done this. I find it disrespectful.

> **Tom:** I agree. Did you notice that when he finally joined us, he didn't apologize? As far as I'm concerned, I've lost some respect for Bill.

> **John:** Me too! Gotta go to another meeting. See ya!

If these workers were to build on the exchange and get beyond criticizing and instead seek a solution where they establish a mutual understanding of how best to work together, it would look like the following:

> **John:** I was really taken aback by how Bill never called us to let us know he would be late for our meeting today.

This is the second time he's done this. I find it disrespectful.

Tom: I agree. Did you notice that when he finally joined us, he didn't apologize? As far as I'm concerned, I've lost some respect for Bill.

John: Me too! You know, maybe what we all need to do moving forward is agree to give each other a call or send a text message if we are going to be more than ten minutes late. That way, we won't all be sitting around doing nothing while we wait for everyone to show up.

Tom: That sounds good to me. You just reminded me that perhaps Bill's real issue is what we experienced when I worked on the Xram project. It was impossible for meetings to start on time because all our meetings were scheduled back-to-back—just as we are currently doing. If you think about it, we leave ourselves no time to check emails or use the facilities. If your first meeting is in another building, there's no way you can get to the next meeting on time. So what we did that worked real well and what we could agree to do now is to start our meetings at ten after instead of on the hour.

John: That makes sense. Let's bring these ideas up to Bill later today and get him to agree. Gotta go to another meeting. See you later!

TASK EXPECTATION PACKAGES ARE ALSO IMPORTANT

It's not only important to establish a Matched Relationship Expectation Package with regard to how to work together. Expectations also need to be clear and mutually understood with regard to communicating tasks and projects. When expectations about a task or project are clearly spelled out and all parties involved keep their commitments, once again, there is less need to criticize.

Become Aware of What You Typically Criticize Others About

Here's a quick but insightful exercise that sheds some light on the reasons we criticize others in the workplace.

Take a moment to reflect on the past two weeks and ask yourself:

► What have I criticized others for?

► What have I wanted to criticize others for but did not?

Write down the situations you've recalled on a sheet of paper so you create one list.

Now, examine your list and see if any patterns exist. If your list resembles those from workshops I've conducted on criticism, you most likely will find that there are three main reasons we criticize or want to criticize others:

Reason #1: Unclear expectations—you left out important information related to your expectations.

Reason #2: Expectations that were not matched—the receiver heard one thing and you as the giver meant another. This is a common misunderstanding.

Reason #3: Expectations that were clearly established were not kept—the receiver knew clearly what to do but didn't deliver.

As Coaching Tip #9 demonstrates, much of the criticism that arises in the workplace is the result of expectations not being clearly communicated from the outset, because the parties involved interpreted what was said differently, or because the parties knew what was to be done but failed to keep their agreement. More succinctly, expectations were either unclear, not matched, or not kept. So once again, to minimize the need for criticism, task expectation packages need to be established and agreements need to be kept. Where, then, does communication typically fall short when delegating tasks?

It's been my experience when assigning tasks that the end result is frequently not communicated. Too much emphasis is placed on "what to do," as in "I need this report typed out"—only to say after the report has been turned in, "This needed to be double-spaced." Not establishing a clear deliverable time is another commonly overlooked mistake or unspoken, as when the boss says, "I need this done by tomorrow." The employee completing the task thinks she has until 5 p.m. the next day, whereas the boss is thinking by midday at the latest. Leaving out information associated with tasks is also a common unspoken that results in having to do rework. To address these common errors, it's important to emphasize that both parties are responsible for making sure that expectations are clearly understood and agreed upon before ending the initial conversation.

One innovative leader of a highly energized team that thrived on doing everything at a fast pace successfully encouraged all his managers to use an egg timer to slow everyone down. Both the managers and their team members were responsible for making sure—within the three-minute period set by the egg timer—that they understood what was to be done, what the end result would look like, when it was due, at what quality, and to whom the task was to be handed off, as well as the importance of the task. Both the managers and the team members could not walk away before the three-minute period ended. This procedure heightened everyone's awareness about the importance of doing the right things correctly the first time around.

CLARIFYING THE BOOK'S PURPOSE

By now, you may have concluded, and rightly so, that the unspoken here is that this book is not promoting more criticism in the workplace or in your life. Quite the opposite. What's being promoted is the need to criticize one another less than we do. The point here is that when unspokens are accurately spotted and when matched expectation packages are mutually understood and upheld, there is less of a need to give and receive criticism!

However, here's another unspoken: Because relationships are dynamic and because human beings aren't perfect, they communicate tasks or ideas poorly, break agreements, fail to remember to do something, and get emotionally upset. This causes them to speak first and think later, and on and on. Given the nature of human beings, the need to give criticism is inevitable. It may be uncomfortable at the moment, but if it's truly meant to be helpful and is taken that way, in the end, relationships will be enhanced.

Creating an atmosphere of acceptance for giving and receiving criticism comes down to this: Dialogues between us and the people we work with, live with, socialize with, and play with should always place importance on understanding one another's expectations. When conflicts arise (and they surely will), awareness of expectations will allow all parties to reflect on where they may have erred. The result will be a new understanding that strengthens trust and respect, enabling the parties to more quickly resolve any differences. Having an atmosphere of acceptance opens the door for more productive exchanges and outcomes and enhances healthy and positive relationships.

Quick Review for Easy Recall

Create an atmosphere of acceptance where the potential for conflict is minimized and criticism is more likely accepted.

1. The first ingredient for creating an atmosphere of acceptance is a mutual level of trust and respect: When there

are high levels of trust and respect, we assume positive intent.

2. The second ingredient is mutually understanding goals and what's personally important: When criticism is linked to goals or what's important to individuals, there's greater acceptance of criticism.

3. The third ingredient is establishing a clear understanding of how best to approach others with criticism: The best way to develop that understanding is by asking.

4. The fourth ingredient is understanding the boundaries that define the relationship: Criticism directly related to work is within allowable bounds provided it comes from a qualified source.

To put the four ingredients to work, you must establish Matched Relationship Expectation Packages with those you work closely with and rely on. A Matched Relationship Expectation Package is a clear, mutually understood, and agreed-upon understanding of what's expected from others and what they can expect from you.

PART TWO

Making the Criticism Exchange Work for You

CHAPTER 4

Delivering Criticism with Confidence in Sensitive Times

> *A coach is someone who can give correction without causing resentment.*[1]
>
> —JOHN WOODEN

Giving criticism to others is difficult because we know that even though it is intended to be helpful, once given, criticism can be taken the wrong way and can even jeopardize the health of a relationship. This is the reason why criticism seems so potentially dangerous and such a delicate form of communication.

This chapter will forever take the gamble aspect out of the criticism you give. It will provide you with the logical tools that enable you to move forward with confidence with the helpful criticism that you give.

BEING PREPARED AS THE GIVER

Proper preparation is the all-important key to giving the kind of criticism that will be accepted and acted upon. As we discussed earlier, many people mistakenly believe that it is the giver who is in control during the criticism exchange, when in actuality it is the receiver. Once criticism is uttered, the receiver has control in the form of decision making over what, if any, action to take. Therefore, it is *before* criticism is delivered that the giver has the most control. This is the preparation phase. During this phase, the giver needs to assess what she knows about the receiver, as well as her reasons for offering criticism. The preparation phase underscores the rubric of *thinking before you speak*!

As you move through the preparation phase, you need to know three things about the person you will be criticizing:

1. Be aware of individual goals and what is important to the person you plan to criticize. An important part of developing the Matched Relationship Expectation Package discussed in Chapter 3 is knowing what a person's goals are or what he considers important within the scope of your relationship. If you lack knowledge of an individual's goals or ambitions, then it is more difficult to present criticism as having any value. Not having this information can mean that your intentions will be questioned.

2. Know the individual's criticism preference. When you are delivering criticism, your feeling of comfort is secondary to that of the receiver. The style and tone of the interaction needs to be in accordance with that person's preferences. As emphasized earlier, it is important that we know how the people we care about, depend upon, and work closely with prefer to be approached. This knowledge eliminates the need to guess and perhaps cause hurt feelings. It's also important to remember that it's the person's preference and not yours that's important. You may prefer a soft approach when someone criticizes you, but some people prefer that it be delivered in a blunt and straightforward way—which means that you need to adapt your approach.

3. Make sure trust and respect is established in your relationship. As part of your preparation phase before delivering criticism, assess the level of trust and respect established in the relationship.

This is because low levels of trust and respect on the part of the receiver equate to a greater probability that the criticism will be misconstrued and perceived as not helpful—or even rejected altogether. Most of us have a pretty good instinct about the level of trust and respect that exists between us and the people with whom we regularly deal, both on and off the job. Past experiences give us the clues that enable us to assess the extent to which others respect our opinions and the integrity behind what we say. But people can respect our judgments and opinions on some subjects more than others. For instance, you may be highly respected for your technical expertise, but when it comes to financial matters, forget it!

COACHING TIP #10:

Have You Thought About the Type of People Who Are Most Difficult to Criticize?

What type of people do you have the most difficulty giving criticism to? Think a moment: Do you find it more difficult to criticize someone of the same sex, or is it more difficult to criticize someone of the opposite sex? Do differences in religion or political views make it more difficult?

A survey of the membership of Women at the Top (WATT), a Tucson, Arizona–based networking organization of women business owners and executives, found that criticizing their boss or a board member was by far the most difficult criticism to give (72 percent said it was "sometimes difficult" or "almost always difficult"). These same women confessed to having difficulty criticizing someone older than themselves (44 percent), as well as having to criticize their peers (43 percent). What was least difficult? Criticizing someone who is younger![2]

While we often don't think about these sensitivities, they do exist and can play a part in whether or not the criticism is accepted. They serve as unspokens and need to be spotted!

Nevertheless, people in the workplace can show respect as a matter of courtesy but quietly harbor mistrust. If you suspect a lack of trust, then you must try to remedy the situation. Take the initiative to clear up issues, and make a concerted effort to nurture the relationship. Otherwise, no matter how helpful your intentions, your criticisms may be met with resistance.

BEING PREPARED WHILE USING THE "GIVER COMMUNICATION CHART"

The Giver Communication Chart introduced in this chapter is your blueprint for giving helpful criticism. You should always refer to this guide in your preparation process. Its purpose is to quickly take you through your plan for maximizing the effectiveness of what you will say. You can trust it and rely on it for any kind of criticism. Once you move through the questions in the chart and assess your true readiness to give a criticism, your confidence will be at or near its peak. The chart will allow you to create a sequenced plan so you do not have to memorize lines and risk coming across as artificial or phony. Furthermore, you will not get caught up in one-size-fits-all messaging. Following a prescriptive approach is ineffective and too limiting. You want your messages to come across genuinely so the receiver recognizes that your intent is positive and meant to be helpful and instructive.

Because the Giver Communication Chart is a process, it applies to all situations on and off the job. Besides helping you during the preparation phase, it will also assist during subsequent conversations with receivers. Interactions occur spontaneously, and the back-and-forth can happen very quickly. You need to make sure you are staying focused and effective on a consistent basis.

When it is time to give criticism, your own comfort too often becomes a priority—and this goal of being comfortable is seldom achieved. Worry not; your focus when delivering criticism is to be effective rather than comfortable. Relying on the Giver Communication Chart ensures a productive exchange. Using it to prepare may take some extra time. However, in the end, it will save you lots of time and potentially any grief that comes with poorly handled criticism. After you refer to it a number of times, it will become second nature to you.

Always keep in mind that giving criticism is a skill. Giving criticism is not unlike working with a sharp tool, like a table saw. It is a pleasure to watch skilled operators use a machine like this. Unskilled users, however, can only hope that they will not lose a finger (in the case of the table saw) or lose a friend, companion, or associate (in the case of criticism). Becoming skillful in giving criticism and recognizing that your purpose is to be helpful overrides any feelings of anxiety. In short, the Giver Communication Chart is your guide for effectively delivering criticism so it's received as intended and conveys that you care about the person.

When you view the Giver Communication Chart for the first time, it may seem overwhelming and appear very complex—but it's really not. What is nice about the chart is that it organizes what you are already thinking and helps to ensure that you do not leave anything out. Most likely, you are already thinking about the timing, the set-ting, the issue at hand, how best to resolve the situation, your own attitude, and the potential receptivity of the receiver. The Giver Communication Chart captures all that and more as it helps get you ready for the actual exchange between you and the receiver. In the end, you'll applaud yourself when you find that the receiver is inspired to take action and address the situation in a timely and effective manner, utilizing the new insights she has gained. When criticism is viewed as a process where there's a two-way exchange, as opposed to a directive or mandate, it becomes a powerful, helpful, and influential tool.

To organize your thinking, the Giver Communication Chart intro-duces three main steps. Each one helps you gather essential informa-tion. Bypassing a step or any part of a step puts the criticism at risk of being rejected or possibly tarnishing the relationship. The Giver Com-munication Chart is shown in Figure 4-1.

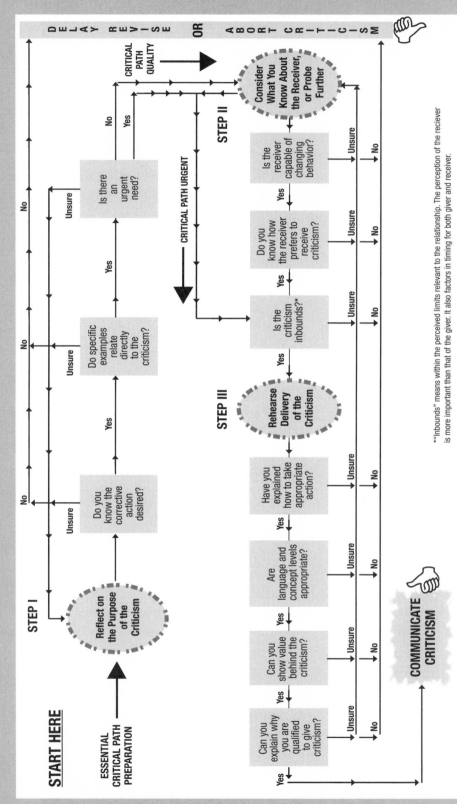

Figure 4-1. THE GIVER COMMUNICATION CHART

*"inbounds" means within the perceived limits relevant to the relationship. The perception of the receiver is more important than that of the giver. It also factors in timing for both giver and receiver.

OVERVIEW OF THE THREE STEPS NECESSARY IN GIVING CRITICISM

STEP I:
Reflect on the Purpose of the Criticism

The first step involves determining the true purpose of your criticism. This is where you gather information. The information gathered needs to genuinely be of help to the receiver.

STEP II:
Consider What You Know About the Receiver, or Probe Further

The second step encourages you to consider what you know about the receiver in an effort to formulate a message that goes beyond the "what" and incorporates the "how." Keep in mind that receivers expect to be criticized. The part they often have trouble with is the "how." They are sensitive to the manner in which the criticism is delivered. Remember, the message needs to convey and the receiver needs to sense that your intent is to help.

STEP III:
Rehearse Delivery of the Criticism

The third step involves mentally rehearsing your delivery. This is a key step because it gives you the opportunity to take the information you've gathered and present it in a tactful and caring way so it is easily understood by the receiver. During your rehearsal, you want to check out whether or not the message is believable, will be perceived as genuine, and is convincing. This is also the point when you deploy mental imagery or visualization, which athletes and actors use just prior to a competition or performance. It is a good technique to use for enhancing performance and, in this case, for ensuring a productive exchange.

Each of the three steps includes a series of questions to ask yourself. Moving along this path from question to question and step to step will bring you increasingly closer to ensuring that the criticism is valid and that positive action can be taken. As you mentally answer each question with "yes," you can move to the next question on the essential critical path, and you are on your way to delivering helpful criticism. However, if your answer to any question is "no," then you want to either delay, revise, or abort the process of delivering the criticism. If you are unsure of any of your answers, reexamine the purpose of the criticism or probe further—whether it means probing yourself or probing the receiver.

THE QUESTIONS YOU NEED TO ASK YOURSELF IN EACH OF THE THREE STEPS

STEP I:
Reflect on the Purpose of the Criticism

As we discussed, you have one clear purpose, which is to take information that's rooted in negativity and deliver it in such a way that informs and inspires a receiver to want to bring about a change in his behavior that will result in resolving whatever issue is at hand.

As you gather information, consider whether or not the receiver can do anything about the criticism. The worst criticism to give someone is the kind that refers to circumstances that are out of the receiver's control. It's the colleague who blurts out without thinking, "It's too bad you didn't go to an Ivy League school" or "You aren't much of a team player because you played an individual sport while in college or high school." Likewise, it's the boss who tells a broad-shouldered, well-built, 6'7", 260-pound manager that he appears too forceful when he walks into a room! Delivering criticism about something the receiver can do nothing about is misdirected and sets off alarm signals to receivers.

Watch out for criticisms where your purpose is unclear. Here's a good example. A manager schedules a morning staff meeting to begin promptly at 9:30. One of his employees walks into the meeting at 9:42. The manager interrupts the meeting and says, as the employee takes his seat, "Well, glad you could join us at 9:42. . . ." Now, what's the manager's purpose here? Obviously, it isn't to let the employee know that the manager can tell time. Indirectly, the manager may have been trying to convey to everyone present the importance of punctuality. All well and good—but if so, the approach was risky because the employee could be seething in embarrassment over what just took place, and he could totally overlook whatever valuable point the manager may have been trying to make.

To ensure that the purpose of the criticism is to bring about a positive outcome, you need to think before you speak. Consider if the corrective action is possible and, if so, ask the questions presented in Figure 4-2.

FIGURE 4-2:
QUESTIONS TO ASK DURING STEP I

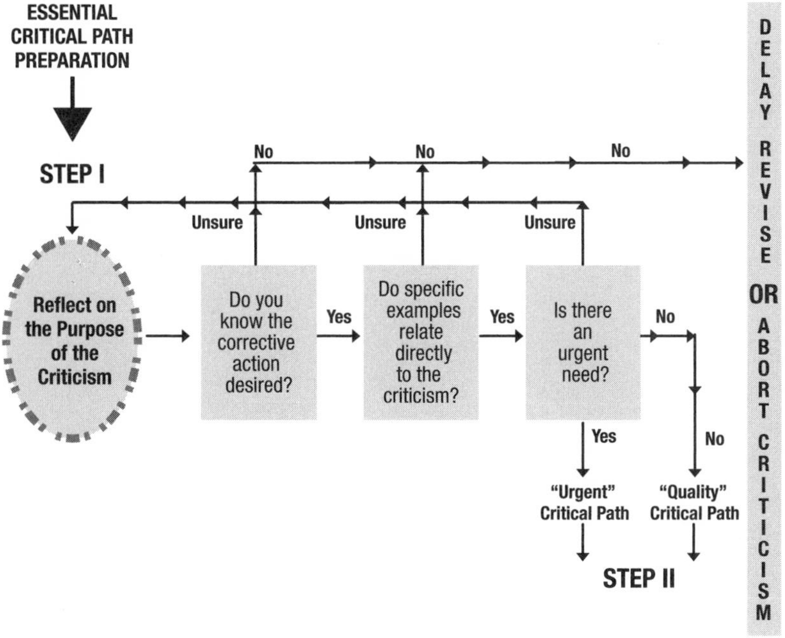

Step I, Question 1: *Do You Know the Corrective Action*
Desired?

Asking this question first positions you well, since it prevents you
from overreacting emotionally. It requires a "yes" or "no" answer, not
an "unsure." Taking the time to answer this question puts the all-
important rule of "thinking before you speak" to work.

Perhaps you can recall the disappointment or frustration you felt
when you found out that a team member failed to follow through on
an assignment that you desperately needed to have done. When
questioning the team member, you received a lame excuse. In a huff,
you blurted out angrily, "How can you offer this stupid excuse? My
kids could come up with a better story than the one you just con-
jured up!"

When stepping back and examining this scene, you may have felt
some satisfaction expressing your quick-draw comment, but what was
the purpose of your criticism? If you think about what you said, nothing has been resolved. The assignment still needs to be done, and the
deadline is still the same. Does the team member know what she
needs to do? Do you know what the desired corrective action is? Pointing out what disturbed you was your only message—and it was not of
any use.

If you don't know what you want the receiver to do differently,
then the Giver Communication Chart advises you to delay, revise, or
abort the criticism entirely. Let's say you have an employee who keeps
giving you PowerPoint decks with errors. You learn that the employee
is trying to proof off the screen, so you suggest that he let some time
go by between finishing the draft and trying to proof it. You even suggest printing the PowerPoint documents in order to catch errors in
the printout. Still, you spot mistakes. You don't know what to do next.
At this point, the Giver Communication Chart directs you to revise
your delivery and explain up front that you don't know what else to
suggest. If you haven't done so already, this is when you engage the
employee directly to help come up with the solution. For criticism to
bring about a positive outcome, receivers need to know specifically
what they should do differently.

Step I, Question 2: *Do Specific Examples Relate Directly to the Criticism?*

We have all been told that it's easier to learn from our mistakes than our successes. Pointing out specific examples helps receivers to learn from their mistakes. When no specifics are presented, receivers start to question whether the giver took any time to understand the circumstances surrounding the criticism. For instance, when a giver says, "From what I can see, you're not playing on the team," the receiver is going to want some specifics to help better understand what he is doing wrong. If the giver cannot provide specifics, the receiver is apt to become suspicious of the purpose behind the criticism and less willing to take appropriate action. The receiver may think there is an ulterior motive on the part of the giver rather than an attempt to be helpful. When receivers think like this, it can weaken the trust relationship.

To have the criticism accepted, you need to ask yourself: "What do all of the facts and examples I have gathered really mean?" It is important to examine whether the examples relate directly back to the criticism you have in mind. Take the lawyer who receives a letter back from his administrative assistant. He notices that there are two misspellings in the letter. One of them is the client's name. The lawyer is infuriated and chastises the assistant for the misspellings. She goes home that night, and when family members ask her how things went during the day, she tells everyone that her boss went ballistic over two simple typographical errors. Now, if you went back to the boss and asked him what really made him angry, he might tell you that it was his assistant's lack of attention to detail and the absence of pride in her work—two important themes that never got communicated to her.

Here's another example: an employee who works very hard throughout the day, yet misses important deadlines. Even when her manager checks in on her, it doesn't always guarantee that specific tasks are getting done each day. Only by stepping back and asking, "What do all these facts mean?" did the manager realize that the real issue is that the employee didn't know how to set priorities appropriately. So be sure to consider your facts and then go one step further and ask your-self if there is a broader picture of what they mean.

Step I, Question 3: *Is There an Urgent Need?*

Some of us may have learned to point out a mistake right at the moment it's spotted. This is misguided advice. To deliver helpful criti-cism, it's valuable to determine if the criticism is urgent or not. When the criticism is urgent, the Giver Communication Chart directs you to bypass the receiver and focus instead on the situation itself, taking corrective action as needed. If criticism is warranted, in most cases, it can be delivered at another time—when there is less tension in the air and when you have time to focus on something other than the issue at hand. This is an important consideration even in the heat of the moment because it forces you to examine whether the expectations have ever been clearly communicated. If you don't know whether the expectations have been clearly expressed, you need to revise any deliv-ery of the criticism. Give the receiver the benefit of the doubt in an effort to ensure that when you criticize in the future, what you say is credible, legitimate, and, most importantly, accepted.

Consider this example. It's late on a Friday afternoon and one of your employees turns in a design she has been laboring over for most of the week. As her boss, you're anxious to look at what she has deliv-ered. You notice errors in her work. Is it urgent to point out those errors immediately, even though the work isn't due yet? What will the outcome be if the situation is not immediately addressed? It's gener-ally a matter of judgment. If you determine that it's not urgent, then you can take some time to factor in how best to approach the receiver about the errors. You may even take time to ask yourself if the receiver has been trained or knows how to fix the errors. You'll also be able to factor in the best timing for you to point out the errors in a helpful way and allow the receiver to view your observations as instructional. It's also worth acknowledging the positive attributes of the submitted work: When you point out the weaknesses, you also want to note the strengths. When asking if the criticism is urgent or not, you will come to realize (depending on your line of work) that most criticisms do not qualify as urgent. Conveniently, this gives you the time to really think through what you want to say and how best to say it, so the receiver understands that you are trying to be helpful. Considering the urgency of a situation is valuable because it forces you to think . . . before reacting emotionally.

COACHING TIP #11:

Consider Whether a Criticism Is Urgent

Take a moment to jot down situations or circumstances in the past three weeks where you've delivered criticism to another person at work. If you'd like, also add to your list those times when you wanted to say something but for some reason decided not to.

_____

_____

_____

_____

_____

_____

_____

Review your list, and ask yourself how urgent each of these situations were. If you are like most managers and nonmanagers, you'll find that a majority of your criticisms are not urgent.

In order for you to reach the conclusion of what's urgent or not urgent, you must have been working with some criteria. Think about the criteria you are using, and ask yourself if they are serving you well. Most criticisms are urgent when the company is at risk of losing a customer or an employee, possibly losing money, or facing a legal or safety-related matter.

STEP II:
Consider What You Know About the Receiver, or Probe Further

In Step II, we move on to what you know about the receiver. Because of the negativity associated with criticism, receivers can be particularly sensitive. As a result, they are often focusing on what is being said but are possibly even more alert to the circumstances surrounding how and when the criticism is delivered. If the giver has not considered the receiver's capacity for change or criticism preference, the receiver may reject the criticism, but in addition, the quality of the relationship may be damaged. So the giver needs to ask the questions found in Figure 4-3.

Figure 4-3.
QUESTIONS TO ASK DURING STEP II

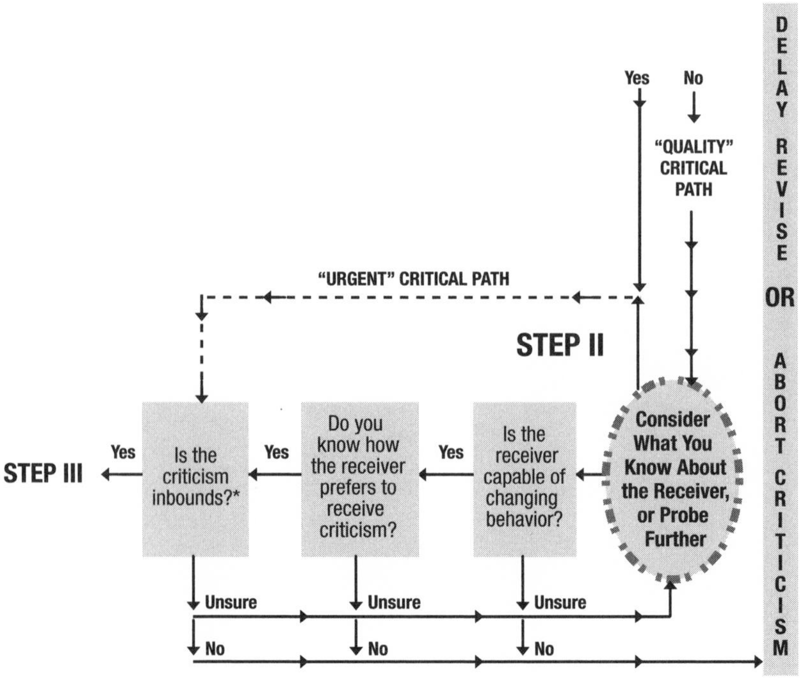

*"Inbounds" means within the perceived limits relevant to the relationship. The perception of the reciever is more important than that of the giver. It also factors in timing for both giver and receiver.

Step II, Question 4: *Is the Receiver Capable of Changing Behavior?*

Have you ever delivered criticism to someone in the workplace only to have her thank you but in the end do nothing about it? If so, it's important to consider if she is capable of doing what's necessary to make the change, interested in making the change, or wants to make the change. Keep in mind that if you are unsure about an answer, you need to examine what you know about the receiver and, if necessary, probe further. This is an important consideration. Criticizing someone who cannot make the changes required only sets the receiver up for continued criticism. The same holds true for someone who doesn't want to change or is resistant to change.

Here's an example that illustrates this point. William is a senior manager with more than two hundred employees in his department and seven direct reports. One of his younger direct reports, Joe, likes to keep up with the latest trends in fashion and hair, and he likes to spike his hair. The only trouble is that he works for a company where everyone dresses and acts very conservatively. Even though there is no policy on spiked hair, William decides that he needs to say something to Joe. William does his best to approach the subject, and Joe listens politely. After several weeks, William realizes that nothing has changed. William makes another attempt, explaining the situation and suggesting that appearance factors could limit Joe's chances for promotion. To William's surprise, Joe says that perhaps he could modify his hair slightly, but he truly prefers to keep the look, even if it means being passed over for promotion. At that point, William drops the issue. Joe is not a customer-facing employee, so the decision is made to respect Joe's wishes.

Sometimes, people are unable to make the change necessary because they are not capable. We're talking, for example, about the technical expert who wants to advance within a company where the simple means of advancement is to move into management. This is done with the technical expert. While his boss's intentions may have been good, it doesn't take long before it becomes apparent that the technical expert lacks the interpersonal skills needed to manage people. All he can do is pass out assignments, and sometimes he even has trouble doing that. The situation is no different in sales. We tend to take the best sales representatives and make them managers. But sometimes, even if higher-ups hand out a good deal of criticism, it won't yield the outcomes desired if the former sales reps aren't suited to management. Lots of time and energy get spent for very little return, and frustration levels mount for everyone involved.

Once it becomes a reality that a person is incapable of or unwilling to change, the Giver Communication Chart guides you out of the process because criticizing no longer serves a purpose. When this occurs, it may signal the need to offer counseling with regard to the deficiency or to take steps to remove the person from that particular responsibility.

What if you are unsure about a person's capabilities? It's acceptable to go directly to the person and ask. This is what Marilyn, the senior editor for a major women's magazine, did. Marilyn had inherited a new assistant, Josephine, by way of a recent reorganization. Josephine continually made grammatical errors. Marilyn frequently pointed out the mistakes and, when time permitted, sometimes gave Josephine a condensed grammar lesson. One day, Marilyn decided to approach Josephine about the reports she was receiving that were loaded with grammatical errors. During their conversation, Josephine admitted that her knowledge of grammar was weak. The discussion concluded with a two-month improvement plan. Both agreed that if satisfactory progress wasn't made, even after a concentrated effort, Josephine would be considered not suited for the job.

Step II, Question 5: *Do You Know How the Receiver Prefers to Receive Criticism?*

Having to criticize is just as much a part of the workplace as having to face tight deadlines or unexpected obstacles. Therefore, the importance of knowing individual criticism preferences cannot be overemphasized. Remember, research has found that receivers expect to be criticized in the workplace. In addition, employees least resent criticism from their boss as compared to from other people in their life. However, no matter the circumstances of the criticism, it's not enough to have established common goals or to know the goals and wishes of the individual. The big stress producer about criticism is "how" it is delivered. As was pointed out in Chapter 3, a common mistake is thinking we can deliver criticism however we choose, then watch for the reaction and make mental notes along the way. This trial-and-error approach is time-consuming and may cause bruises along the way.

The most accurate and meaningful method of giving criticism is to begin by asking the person how he would prefer to be criticized. Getting the purest and most reliable information involves asking the person directly. While it may take people a few minutes to warm up to such a question, in all likelihood, they have a pretty good idea of how, when, and from whom they willingly accept criticism.

Don't simply rely on behavioral instruments or assume that you know because you believe you have great instincts about people. Actually asking shows that you respect individuals and are interested in who they are and what their preferences are. And, oh yes, you can bet they will appreciate the question. Why? Because people like to talk about themselves.

Unless you are a coach, drill sergeant, or director of a play, receivers typically are not likely to be responsive to givers who yell, use profanity, or frequently repeat the same criticism. Watch out for pointing fingers in the receiver's face. Also, one of the biggest turnoffs is the giver's tone of voice, so pay special attention to yours. Keeping your tone matter-of-fact avoids conveying a number of unspokens that are often perceived by receivers as put-downs. All of these factors can result in the criticism being perceived as outside what's acceptable in the relationship. (There is more about out-of-bounds criticism in the section on Question 6.)

What if you don't know the person because you just met at work or the person is someone you don't deal with regularly, such as a waiter or sales clerk? When you don't know, the Giver Communication Chart advises that you revise, delay, or abort the criticism altogether. If an objective is to develop a relationship, as with a new employee, you may elect to wait. However, if the situation involves your waiter or sales clerk, chances are great you don't want to wait, nor are you interested in developing a long-term relationship, so you say what displeases you with the anticipation that the issue gets resolved.

If you elect not to wait because you believe you are faced with a situation where you need to deliver criticism to someone you don't know, you can approach the subject cautiously, while simultaneously remaining flexible to revise your delivery as you pick up clues from the receiver. You could start the conversation by saying, "We haven't worked together long enough to really get to know one another, and a situation has come up that needs to be addressed. In the spirit of getting our relationship off to a good start, I'd like to know if you want me to get right to the point, or do you want me to ease into the topic and provide some background information?" At the least, you are engaging the receiver at this point and are attempting to establish a mutual understanding around how best to approach the person. It takes about forty-five seconds to set the stage.

Notice that the Giver Communication Chart provides you with the option to skip this question if the circumstances are urgent and warrant it. By doing this, however, you have to realize that you are not operating with the best information, which leaves your criticism vulnerable to rejection.

Determining how best to interact with another person is analogous to an architect's blueprint. It needs to be tweaked and adjusted before everything begins to fit. Besides, we are dealing with humans, and sometimes what people say they "want" isn't what they need. So there's nothing wrong with going back and forth a few times to work things out. That way, receivers know that what's being communicated is intended to help. This is an essential part of the "skill" associated with giving helpful criticism.

After engaging in a difficult conversation, make it a practice to go back to the person at a calm moment and address how well each party handled the engagement. That way, you make sure that your Matched Relationship Expectation Package is operative. If you are a team leader or a manager, the onus is on you to initiate these conversations.

COACHING TIP #12:

How to Further Strengthen a Person's Confidence When Criticizing

Maintaining a person's confidence when criticizing is essential. Have you ever thought about what you can do to keep someone's confidence from being rattled? Here are a few tried-and-true approaches:

- ► During the criticism exchange, make it known that it's just a criticism and not a personal annihilation of the individual. Do this by making your belief in the person "spoken" by simply saying outright, "I believe in you."

- ► After criticizing the person, give her the same or a similar task to perform. Now actions are more powerful than words to convey your belief in the individual.

- ► Engage the receiver in the discussion about how best to move forward. Asking her how best to approach correcting the situation says in the unspoken, "I believe in you and respect what you have to say."

- ► Ask the receiver what obstacles or difficulties she anticipates encountering that would cause her concern and possibly jeopardize her being successful. Address each concern by coming up with a workable plan that the receiver believes in.

- ► To convey to the person that the mistake made is behind her and a thing of the past, take notes during the discussion. At the end of the conversation, hold up the sheet of paper and ask her, "Is there anything else we need to discuss about this situation?" If she says "yes," it's a good thing you asked. However, most likely, the receiver will say "no." At that point, rip up the sheet of paper, throw it in a wastepaper basket, and say, "Let's move on from here." What's important is to "absorb the mistake and remember the lesson."

> ► At the end of the criticism exchange and before ending the conversation, change the subject. For example, you could say, "How was your ski trip?" or "Tell me about your son's graduation." Changing the subject sends the message that things are okay between us, even though we had to address a situation.

Step II, Question 6: *Is the Criticism Inbounds?*

Not knowing what receivers consider to be allowable issues for criticism is not unlike walking through a minefield without knowing where the mines are. These days, people can be extremely sensitive to certain kinds of criticism. So before you criticize anyone, even though you have only helpful intentions, be sure—very sure—that you are aware of the boundaries within which your relationship operates. When we speak of boundaries, we are talking about matters that can involve "none-of-your-business" issues and "I-don't-have-to-take-that-from-you" issues. Key boundaries to consider when giving criticism are the appropriateness of content, timing, and place.

Content Boundaries Content is a major consideration when determining whether a criticism is inbounds. Ask yourself: Does the criticism fit within the mutually understood goals and expectations established by the giver and the receiver? This is where creating an atmosphere of acceptance is so important because not only are you accepting criticism in the relationship and clarifying expectations about how best to engage in a productive criticism exchange, but you are also establishing the boundaries within which certain kinds of criticism are allowable or not allowable.

Relationships are surrounded by both spoken and unspoken expectations. If you bring up something that is outside the parameters of the established expectations, then the criticism runs the risk of being rejected because it's out of bounds.

Here's another valuable tip. If you feel queasy or have second thoughts about giving a criticism, it's probably a signal that you are dealing with concerns about whether or not a criticism is inbounds.

The receiver can summarily regard criticism as out of bounds based on the giver's questionable eligibility or lack thereof. For instance, in the workplace, can an employee criticize his boss, or will the boss reject the criticism because she doesn't believe that an employee is at a proper level to criticize? Similarly, team members might believe that because they are on a team together, it must be okay to criticize one another. However, when they do, they might be surprised to find that one of the teammates is not receptive. It's not uncommon for a team member to think, "I only accept criticism from my boss. My boss is the one who does my performance review, not you." This may sound a little harsh, but that's the reality. Team members can't automatically assume that because they are peers, criticizing one another is acceptable. Matters such as this need to be discussed and established so that all have a mutual understanding of how they want to work together.

Timing Boundaries The timing referred to here is from the perspective of both the giver and the receiver. Timing is not to be confused with the urgency of the criticism, which deals more with the nature of a situation. As you might conclude, when a situation is clearly urgent, it overrides any preferences of both givers and receivers. However, when dealing with typical workday situations, if the giver finds himself in a bad mood, feeling pressured, or pressed for time, then delivering criticism might be best classified as being momentarily out of bounds and needing to be delayed. Of course, who isn't pressed for time these days? So when something comes up that requires some helpful criticism, givers need to make the time to meet with the person needing criticism, as opposed to simply putting it off. Standing weekly or biweekly one-on-one meetings are an opportune time to have these conversations.

If you are unsure about the timing, you should probe or ask the receiver. Here's an example of how one regional sales manager for a large pharmaceutical company came around to asking about timing issues. For the past ten years, as regional sales manager, Jake made a point of going out into the field calling on customers with his local sales reps. At the end of his routine monthly visits, while being driven to the airport, he would provide each sales rep with feedback. This routine worked well for years as the sales reps were receptive to his feedback. An exception occurred one day when Jake engaged one young rep named Tony. Each time Jake would provide feedback to Tony, Tony would get defensive and highly argumentative. Jake was concerned because he saw this behavior only when he actually went out on a sales call with Tony. After talking the situation over with a friend, Jake decided to ask Tony what was going on. To Jake's amazement, Tony confessed that his excitement level went through the roof when he made a sale, especially when Jake was on the call with him. Coincidentally, that had occurred during each of the last four visits. Tony further explained that when he received feedback immediately following the call, he was too hyped up, not really listening, and was reactive to any criticisms that Jake brought up. After learning about this, Jake simply decided to hold his feedback sessions with Tony until later in the evening or the first thing the next morning. Jake's timing seemed to have worked and Tony came to appreciate Jake's sensitivity.

Place Boundaries What about place? A good practice, as opposed to a hard-and-fast rule, is to always try to make criticism a private matter.

That's not what happened between Steve and Kerri. While they have known each other for ten years, it's been only recently that Steve has reported directly to Kerri. What's the issue? Kerri conducts their weekly one-on-one meeting in her office cubicle, where there are no walls. Space is at a premium, and Kerri thought nothing of conducting their meetings in her cubicle. The only problem is that people at neighboring desks can hear their conversations. The conversations get quite loud as a result of the combination of Steve and Kerri's passion for what they do and their familiarity with one another. Kerri's criticisms of Steve can also get loud, and everyone nearby tunes in. Then the rumor mill runs wild, as everyone in the department knows what's going on between Steve and Kerri. Rather than let his frustration build, Steve brought up his concern to Kerri. After having the discussion, they scramble each week to schedule one of the limited numbers of conference rooms for their meeting.

While this example may seem obvious, it raises the importance of giving consideration to where best to meet with people. Depending on the situation and the person involved, it might be best to meet outside the workplace in a casual setting where there's less chance of being interrupted. But meeting outside the workplace may not be appropriate with certain people. In fact, it may seem too private! Thus, this is another area where personal judgment comes into play. The thing to keep in mind—always—is the need to think long and hard before criticizing in public.

Considering whether a criticism is inbounds is a crucial question to answer accurately. Remember, if you don't know the answer, you need to revise, delay, or abort the criticism altogether. If you are unsure, you need to probe further.

STEP III:
Rehearse Delivery of the Criticism

Now that you have considered the criticism itself, have decided that your purpose to help is legitimate, and have sorted out how best to approach the receiver, it's time to mentally practice your delivery. This is the work of Step III (see Figure 4-4). To enhance performance, many people in the workplace, just as in sports, rely on mental imagery or visualization techniques. You want to apply these same techniques to delivering criticism. Rehearsing your delivery helps you uncover subtle signs you may be making, such as a sigh or shifting of the eyes, that can cause the receiver to question your intentions. Rehearsing also helps to build your confidence and ensures that you deliver the criticism in the most effective way. You might rehearse timing, tone of voice, expression of delivery, focus, and control. Criticism that conveys guilt, disappointment, or even rejection can have an extremely negative outcome, so be sure to check your delivery to exclude these nonproductive messages. Even though it may take some extra time up front, in the long run, it saves time if you re-hearse your delivery so you feel confident in what you have to say and know how to best say it.

Figure 4-4.
QUESTIONS TO ASK DURING STEP III

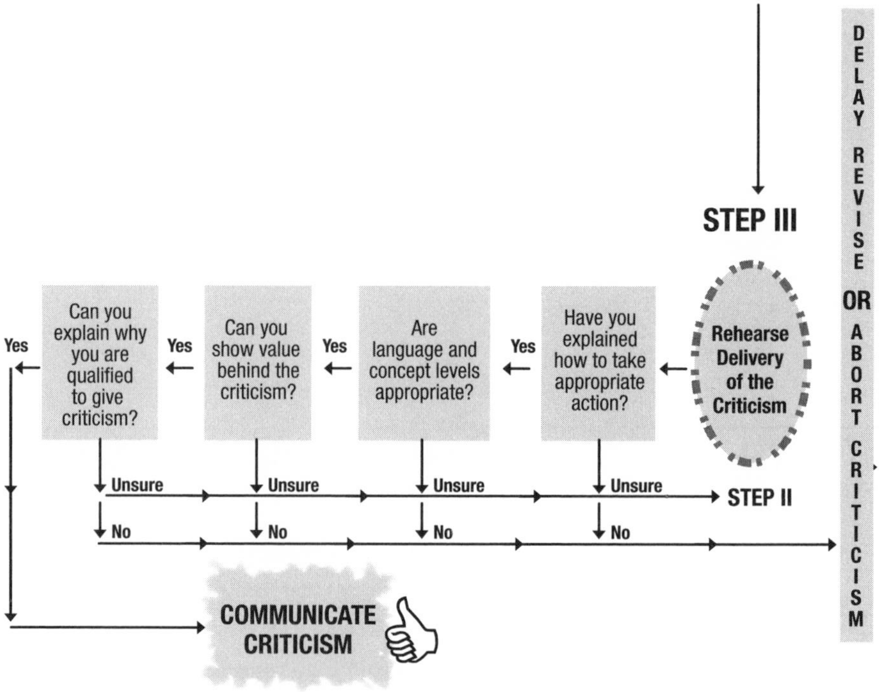

Can practicing guarantee that your criticism will be effective? Not always, but it can improve your chances of creating positive results! Do you always have to practice? If we "think before we speak," then "thinking" equates to "practicing," and so the answer is "yes." What you want to avoid as much as possible is being impulsive. When mentally rehearsing your delivery of criticism, it is important that you consider the questions in Step III.

Step III, Question 7: *Have You Explained How to Take Appropriate Action?*

This question is similar to the first one asked in Step I, where you needed to stop yourself long enough to ask if you knew what you wanted from the receiver. You are revisiting this question here because now you are wondering whether you can explain how to go about correcting or addressing the situation.

Even if you know the specific actions the receiver needs to take, it's valuable to engage her in the discussion of what to do because it sends the receiver an important unspoken message that conveys your respect for her. Asking, "How would you assess the way you handled the situation, and what would you do differently?" provides the receiver with the opportunity to examine the situation on par with the giver, as opposed to feeling talked down to, which is something receivers find unsettling regardless of their years of work experience. By having an open two-way exchange, you are building the person's confidence because you are in essence saying to her, "I believe in you and respect what you have to say." During the exchange, both of you are directing your energies toward a solution and, in the process, your relationship becomes stronger. By making sure the focus is on specifying what the receiver can do, you turn the criticism into a motivational tool for enhancing performance. Furthermore, you will gain the receiver's trust and respect, which also strengthens your relationship. Also, if you don't know what it will take to correct the situation, you need to reveal that right now you don't have a corrective solution, and you invite the receiver's thoughts in that regard.

Never make the mistake of thinking that the mere delivery of the criticism provides the explanation of what the receiver should do next. That's a bad practice! Take, for example, the employee who needs to prioritize his work better. Telling him that he needs to do a better job of setting priorities is helpful. But consider that if the employee knew *how* to prioritize his work appropriately, he would likely do it. Similarly, many managers receive criticism for not participating more in meetings. In all likelihood, if the managers knew how to participate more in meetings, they would. In each situation, it's necessary to explore further the specific actions that the receiver can perform in order to improve things. For instance, the boss could say, "What I mean by participating more in meetings is to go beyond coming prepared. What I'd like you to do is come up with one idea or introduce one good question to raise to the group. Also, if the meeting goes off track, I'd like you take it upon yourself to get everyone back on point."

Providing these insights offers clarity and saves the receiver a lot of time. Most importantly, it avoids having the receiver run the risk of guessing incorrectly. The receiver in this case would view the intentions of the boss as helpful guidance rather than simply as faultfinding.

It's valuable to mention that in some cases, high-level executives believe that once managers reach a certain level, they need only to be made aware of an issue, and from there it's up to them to find the solution. After all, the executives think, certain expectations are associated with particular levels. However, a point worth considering is that with the shortage of leaders today and with the number of leaders coming from all parts of the world, perhaps this long-held belief—especially as it relates to criticism—needs to be revisited.

Here's the point: Be sure to speak mostly about what the receiver can do differently to improve the situation as opposed to bickering over who said what and when. The past is the past and can't be changed, but it can be used as an example. To keep the conversation flowing and to avoid getting derailed, keep the conversation focused on what the receiver needs to do moving forward. When this happens, you are turning the criticism into a motivational tool for enhancing performance and building better relationships.

Step III, Question 8: *Are Language and Concept Levels Appropriate?*

When a conversation involving a criticism begins, receivers' antennae go up and their hearing becomes superanalytical. They become intensely sensitive to facial expressions, tone of voice, word choice, posture, and the general nature of the giver's delivery. None of us likes to feel as if we are being talked down to. It is highly important for givers to avoid being condescending when speaking to receivers or to avoid going over their head. Givers need to take into account receivers' level of experience, education, and cultural background. Here is an incident regarding this that is worth remembering: One resourceful small-business owner of a fire extinguisher company in New York City was discussing a concern he had with a young female employee about her lack of organizational skills. The employee could barely read and had very little schooling. Nevertheless, she was a loyal, hard worker. To help her understand the importance of being organized, he framed the criticism in terms of motherhood. He said, "A mother raising one child doesn't have to be quite as organized as a mother raising three children, but mothers who are organized can do their work more easily." Coming from a large family, she could easily relate to the example.

Be sure to watch out for inflammatory words that can cause sparks to fly, such as "you," "should," "must," "stupid," "idiot," "lazy," and "always." I could list more, but why go on? You get the picture! Barking out these words without gearing your message to a particular receiver can color the motive behind your criticism and cause doubt about your true and helpful purpose.

Using appropriate language and related examples can truly make a difference. If you ignore this, it can hinder receivers' understanding and even rattle their confidence. This was the case with Maria, a young and highly motivated employee seeking to advance in her career. Her boss, Connie, is a top executive in a company of mostly male decision makers. She is sympathetic to Maria's desire to advance and does what she can to mentor Maria. During one of their mentoring sessions, Maria confesses that she crumbles and loses her self-confidence when people say they are disappointed in her. Months later, Maria failed to do something, which upset Connie and spurred her to say those dreaded words, "I'm so disappointed in you." For weeks following that comment, Maria did whatever she could to avoid contact with Connie. Not an ideal outcome, to say the least.

When softening your words—for instance, by saying, "Have you thought about trying this?" "Let me make a suggestion," "Here's some advice," or "Can I offer you some feedback?"—be sure to tell recipients the full story. In other words, let them know you expect them to make a change. Otherwise, you are misleading them, and over time, you risk losing credibility when you bring up the topic again after nothing has improved.

Here's a valuable tip that skilled givers use to further ensure their message is understood: Tailor the message according to whether the receiver's learning style tends to be predominantly visual, auditory, or kinesthetic. Everyone receives and records information using their senses. Sometimes, people prefer one sense over another, even though they can use more than one of their senses to grasp or receive information.

Years ago, I was asked to observe the University of Michigan's basketball team because they were having some problems with a few freshman players. The head coach requested that I attend a workout session to watch the players in action. One player, Rob, was always being criticized for messing up the drills. The head coach felt that Rob was obstinate and a wise guy, and there was thought of dropping him from the team. As I watched Rob go through the elaborate drills that the head coach was explaining verbally to the team, I asked the assistant coach, "Where did Rob come from?" The assistant coach told me that Rob was from a low-income area in southern Florida, where he had been raised by an aunt. It struck me that given Rob's background, perhaps it was inaccurate to describe his attitude as uncooperative. In all likelihood, Rob had grown up playing basketball in the streets, not in a well-equipped gym, and had probably never had a coach watching his every move and telling him what to do next. He had most likely learned to play by watching and then imitating the best players in his neighborhood. Therefore, it might have been difficult for him to grasp the coach's rapid verbal instructions.

After the workout, I mentioned my theory to the two coaches. They decided to modify the way they presented the drills to see what would happen. At the next practice, the head coach first diagrammed the drills on a flip chart and then supplemented this with a verbal explanation. Then he asked Rob and a few other players to demonstrate the drill. The new procedure worked. Rob easily learned the drills and from that time on was perceived by the coaches to be more "cooperative."

So when you are communicating with someone who is visual, you want to use words to create a picture and say, "How does it look to others when you walk in late in the morning?" For the auditory person, you would adjust your message by saying, "What do you think others would say when you walk in late?" For the receiver who is more oriented toward feelings, you would modify your message and say, "When you strut into the office and are late, how do you think that makes others feel?"

Step III, Question 9: *Can You Show Value Behind the Criticism?*

Failing to show value or the benefit associated with the criticism is a common mistake well worth avoiding. When you show value, it helps to legitimize the criticism in the eyes of receivers because they can readily see your purpose as helpful, and then they are much more willing to accept and act upon the criticism.

How can you show value? The only way is to refer back to the Matched Relationship Expectation Package and be sure you can answer the questions below. If you can't answer any of these questions, then you need to revise your delivery or delay the criticism altogether if it's not urgent.

- ► Do you know what's important to this individual?

- ► Do you know the individual's short- and long-term goals?

- ► Have you discussed and mutually agreed upon departmental and divisional goals?

Take what you know, whether it's what's important to the individual or mutually set departmental goals, and link it to the criticism. For instance, let's say respect from others is important to your employee, who comes to weekly staff meetings ten to fifteen minutes late. Showing value would involve your saying, "When you come in ten to fifteen minutes late, how do you think that fosters respect among your peers?"

Let's look at a situation involving Corina, a young engineer who for the past five years has been a star manager. Her goal is to move into middle management, and much to her delight, she has the support of her boss, Ike, and that of Ike's boss. Ike recognizes that while Corina is very good at motivating her team, she does a poor job involving her peers in some of the broader projects, where they could contribute something of value. Ike could tell her that she needs to reach out to her peers more and give them an opportunity to feel part of a project's success. He could even suggest a few key people Corina could talk with to get started. But what's still missing is the value of the criticism. Here's the same criticism presented so it has value: "Corina, you said that you want to advance within the company. Keep in mind that if you want to move up in the organization, there are some unspoken elements that you need to pay attention to, and one of them is having others want you to be a success. At some point, your peers may be reporting to you. If you want their full support, you need to make sure that you involve them when working on various projects so that they have a part to play in the project's success."

If you can't figure out the value to be gained by bringing up the criticism, then the Giver Communication Chart directs you to consider delaying the criticism, saying nothing at all, aborting the whole idea, or revising how you are going to approach the receiver. When you communicate the criticism and the message is perceived by the receiver as having some value, then you have effectively used criticism as a powerful influencing tool for motivating receivers to take action.

Step III, Question 10: *Can You Explain Why You Are Qualified to Give Criticism?*

The reason this is the last question is because it's typically the first thing that receivers ask themselves: "Who is this person and will I accept what she has to say?" It's a last check that your criticism will be considered inbounds now that it has been refined to the point of readiness for delivery. When mentally preparing, ask yourself if you are qualified to deliver the criticism. Asking this question encourages you to consider whether you have the authority or the responsibility for the final outcome of the task or project. In other words, if you have the authority, then you are considered inbounds. This applies when you are dealing with bosses, project leaders, parents, and mates. Experience and expertise also qualifies you and places you inbounds.

However, having the authority and being skilled may not be enough. Take this common off-the-job example, which makes the point very clearly, and chances are great you've experienced it yourself. You are a parent with an excellent driving record, so you decide to teach your teenage son how to drive. However, every time you say something to him while he's driving, sparks go off. After several clashes, you decide to send him to driver-education classes to learn how to drive, even though you know the driving instructor will be giving instructions similar to yours.

Let's return to the workplace and deal with an employee who has body odor. Several employees have brought the issue up to the boss and have claimed that they have difficulty working under such conditions. The boss, a young female manager, decides that it's an issue she needs to address. After all, she is responsible for the work environment, so in her opinion, it is inbounds for her to say something. However, because the employee happens to be a young single man, the manager wonders whether she is the best person to deliver the message. She believes it may be too embarrassing a topic for her to bring up to the employee. Instead, she asks one of his peers, who is close friends with the employee, to mention something. He agrees, and the situation is resolved.

Let's modify the situation by having the following occur: The employee with body odor learns that it was the boss who set up the whole scene. He confronts her and complains that she did not come to him directly. What does the manager do now? Referring back to the Giver Communication Chart, she recalled when considering Step III that she was not the best qualified person to deliver the criticism. This insight helped her when responding to the employee, saying, "I didn't think I was the best person to deliver the message, and yet the message needed to be communicated. So I asked a close friend of yours to deliver the message because it was my attempt to make what I believed to be a sensitive issue more acceptable." Besides conveying that her intent was positive, she apologizes for her faulty approach and thanks the employee for letting her know. If there are issues in the future, she will come to him directly.

Here's a valuable clue that can provide an insight about whether or not you're qualified to give criticism: If no action has been taken after several attempts, then you want to examine whether you are the best person to influence the receiver. That's what I ended up doing when a boss asked me to coach his management team one-on-one. The boss was a strong believer in executive coaching. He had benefited greatly from his own coaching experience and wanted to give his five direct reports the same opportunity. It was their first coaching experience, and four of the managers had a positive response and showed improvements. One manager, though, was resistant, so I decided to bring up the topic with him. After a frank discussion, we learned that the two of us had some mutual experiences. This gave me credibility with him so that he could accept and, most importantly, act upon the critical comments that I had delivered. What's key is making sure that the receiver is willing to take whatever action is necessary to move things forward in a positive manner.

ALL SYSTEMS GO! READY TO DELIVER CRITICISM

After answering each of the questions in the Giver Communication Chart, you are ready to deliver the criticism. While it may have taken you some time at the outset to gather and organize your thoughts before saying anything, in the long run using the Giver Communication Chart will save you time. Why? Because your message will be received as intended, acted upon in a timely manner, help resolve the situation, and over time strengthen relationships. When helpful criticism is viewed as a learning process, it becomes a powerful influencing tool. It's also a "thumbs-up" approach to building trust, respect, and credibility in relationships.

Quick Review for Easy Recall

As the giver, think before you speak, because once you deliver the criticism, the control shifts to the receiver. Thinking before you speak is equivalent to "proper preparation," which equates to following three steps in the Giver Communication Chart.

Step I: Reflect on the purpose of your criticism.

    1. Do you know the corrective action desired?

    2. Do specific examples relate directly to the criticism?

    3. Is there an urgent need?

Step II: Consider what you know about the receiver, or probe further.

    4. Is the receiver capable of changing behavior?

    5. Do you know how the receiver prefers to receive criticism?

    6. Is the criticism inbounds?

Step III: Rehearse delivery of the criticism.

    7. Have you explained how to take appropriate action?

    8. Are language and concept levels appropriate?

    9. Can you show value behind the criticism?

    10. Can you why you are qualified to give criticism?

If the answer to all questions is "yes," move to the next step: Deliver the criticism. If the answer to any question is "no," delay, revise, or abort the criticism. If you are unsure of an answer to any question, reexamine the purpose of the criticism or probe further.

CHAPTER 5

Receiving Criticism

You Have More Control
Than You Think

> *True friends stab you in the front.*[1]
>
> —OSCAR WILDE

J ust as giving criticism is a skill that must be learned, so too is receiving criticism. The two processes differ greatly when it comes to readiness and preparation. Givers of criticism have time and leeway to prepare and even script themselves. Receivers are usually in a "real-time" mode, having to respond effectively without benefit of planning. Criticism can come to us out of the blue at any time or place, and for a reason we may never have imagined. How we react to it and how we utilize our control can be a huge determining factor in the health and well-being of our relationships at work, at home, or among our friends. On either side of the interchange, we must be keenly aware of potential consequences should we overreact, underreact, or allow a criticism to create a brouhaha between ourselves and those we interact with.

CRITICISM CAN COME OUR WAY AT ANY TIME WHEN WE LEAST EXPECT IT

A terrific example of handling criticism as a receiver took place a long time ago in a small London theater on the opening night of George Bernard Shaw's *Arms and the Man*, which was one of Shaw's earliest plays. As you might know, he later wrote *Pygmalion*, which was the basis for the smash Broadway musical *My Fair Lady*. But *Arms and the Man* was Shaw's first commercial success in a career that encompassed sixty-five plays and a half century. As the curtain closed that night, an ecstatic audience hailed Shaw as he came onstage. Applause rained down as the playwright took his bows. As the roars of enthusiasm began to die down, a loud "boo" was heard coming from what seemed to be a lone heckler in the audience. Instantly, the theater became deadly silent as everyone wondered what Shaw would do or say. He remained silent for a few minutes and then, without a tinge of anger, said, "My dear fellow, I quite agree with you, but what are we two against so many?"[2] The audience then cheered with delight and Shaw took another bow. His witty rejoinder well illustrates that it is the receiver who is in control and can set the mood during the criticism process.

Let us now depart the theater and move to a more familiar scene, the modern-day workplace. Phil has just joined a Northeast-based manufacturing company as vice president of the product development group. He calls Marie and Josh, his two direct reports, into his office. They have been working jointly on a new product launch that is positioned to capture a market the company is strategically interested in entering. They, like others on their team, are exhausted because of the long hours they've been working to get everything done to meet the company's ambitious deadlines. Keeping this background information in mind, let's examine the following exchange:

Phil: Hey, guys, thanks for coming in at such short notice. *(In an attempt to break the ice, he makes the following joking remarks.)* By the way, Marie, I didn't know you went to Arizona State. Isn't that a party school? Hey, I'll bet you had a good time there!

(There is general laughter.) Sometime, I'll find out what made you decide to go to that school! *(There is more laughter.)* Anyway, guys, I need to talk to you about budgets and all the design changes you've been making. We simply can't be making all these last-minute changes. You should have worked more closely with engineering at the outset. Besides, it's costly. We simply can't operate without sticking to the budget. Just last week, I had to defend your actions to my boss—and it wasn't easy. I'm counting on both of you to make sure we maintain high quality while keeping costs under control.

Marie: Phil, like you, Josh and I want to maintain high quality and cost-effectiveness. Frankly, we need your help. We could do a better job of inspecting parts, as well as raw materials coming in from our suppliers. If we could meet with you regularly each week to review these and other issues as they arise, that would be helpful. That way, I think we could do a better job of cost containment. What do you think of our meeting more regularly in order to keep better track of the budget?

Phil: Good suggestion! Marie, why don't you make sure we all meet each week.

(Phil's phone rings and he excuses himself, gesturing for Marie and Josh to leave. Outside Phil's office, Josh commends Marie for the way she handled the situation.)

Josh: I do not know how you did it, Marie. I almost lost my temper when Phil said he had to defend our actions to his boss. After all, he's a major source of our frustration! Phil is never available, and we can't do anything without his approval. You certainly handled that situation tactfully. I wish I could control myself as well as you do.

Both Marie's reaction to Phil and George Bernard Shaw's reaction to his heckler demonstrate the most crucial aspect of the entire criticism process—that control of the process lies not with the givers but with the receivers of criticism.

Most of us can recall at least one occasion when a criticism turned a good relationship into a tense one. In retrospect, it is often unclear whether the blame for the potential fracture in the relationship rested with the person who expressed criticism or the one who received it. In either case, it may have had much to do with failing to think before speaking.

In this chapter and Chapter 6, you'll learn how to capitalize on the control that's inherently yours as the receiver. The skills and insights introduced will unquestionably help empower you when you are a receiver of criticism. You'll learn how to assess whether a criticism warrants acceptance or rejection. Like a laser, you'll see through the chaos of emotions that so often accompany criticism to determine if it's intended to be helpful or not. In fact, exercising control also encompasses using your emotions as an asset. Just like Marie in the scene with Phil, you will learn how to optimize your position in a conversation involving criticism, even when it comes from an unskilled giver.

Specifically, this chapter introduces a thinking process that you can silently use to enable you to easily determine whether the giver's intention, above all else, is to be helpful. You will gain the necessary confidence to determine whether to accept the criticism and do something about it or reject it altogether. This thinking tool is the Receiver Control Chart. Used as a convenient reference, it asks you a series of questions designed to help position you to benefit when you're in the role of criticism receiver—a role that can otherwise induce feelings of helplessness and uncertainty.

Follow these guidelines and you will be more receptive and more willing to listen to what others say without feeling threatened or needing to immediately lash out in self-defense. As Steve Maraboli, author of *Life, the Truth, and Being Free*, tells his audiences, "Incredible change happens in your life when you decide to take control of what you do have power over instead of craving control over what you don't."[3] Or, as one of America's most beloved songwriters, Irving Berlin, is reported to have said, "Life is 10 percent what you make it and 90 percent how you take it." In your case, it's tapping into what can happen in your life when you exercise the control that's inherently yours as the receiver of criticism.

To begin our empowering journey in how to benefit as the receiver of criticism, let's revisit a few insights presented in Chapter 2. These points will help us recognize what Marie and even George Bernard Shaw did when they found themselves on the firing line.

- ► Criticism is rooted in negativity. That alone is stress producing and causes discomfort. Furthermore, the giver is pointing out negative aspects of our behavior, statements, or beliefs through an expression of nonapproval. The challenge is that we can't let it throw us. Furthermore, givers think they are right; they have the power of their convictions, be they correct or incorrect.

- ► As the receiver, you determine how you want to listen. You can use your control to listen for "what" is being said as you bypass "how" the criticism is being delivered. In Marie's case in the example earlier in this chapter, she could have become irritated because she didn't like being referred to as one of the "guys." She could also have let herself get upset at her boss's sarcastic tone of voice when he was talking about where she went to college.

- ► You can also elect to listen to understand, as opposed to listen to argue and judge, by being more attentive to "what" is being said in an effort to understand where the giver is coming from. You can elect to ignore information that's not relevant. Once again, Marie chose not to say anything about Phil's comments about her college days. Rather than interpret his comment about Arizona State as a criticism or even an insult, she decided to let it go because she viewed what he said as a poor attempt at levity. As with Marie, the choice is yours.

- ► Exercising control also includes making sure you know what specific actions to take that are in line with the giver's intent. Marie did that well.

► Very importantly, keeping an open mind and operating with positive intent positions you to learn something of value from the criticism. I am reminded of a valuable insight that comes from a seventeenth-century author of maxims and memoirs, François de La Rochefoucauld, when he said, "Few people have the wisdom to prefer the criticism that would do them good, to the praise that deceives them."[4]

Gaining "some good" from criticism involves learning to employ the Receiver Control Chart.

THE "RECEIVER CONTROL CHART"

This chart is your reference tool for keeping an open mind. It will help train you to effectively process what's being said. The chart is based on the reality that critical commentary is merely information that you need to sift through to determine whether the criticism is intended to be helpful or not. Rather than feel helpless, you can use the Receiver Control Chart to help you engage in a worthwhile dialogue to identify the potential value to be gained from the criticism. More specifically, you are exercising your control to make sure that the information you are getting is valid, that you understand clearly the suggested corrective action, that it has value to you, and that the overall message is well intended and likely to lead to a positive outcome. Keep in mind that at any point, you can silently reject the criticism. But before you do, you must ponder the potential consequences of not accepting it.

Another purpose of the Receiver Control Chart is to help you de-emotionalize the criticism. Keeping your emotions in check helps you to listen as opposed to tuning out. Avoiding a strong emotional charge will help you better sort out the intentions behind the criticism and keep the faultfinding in proper perspective so you can position yourself to benefit from what is being communicated. The Receiver Control Chart is shown in Figure 5-1.

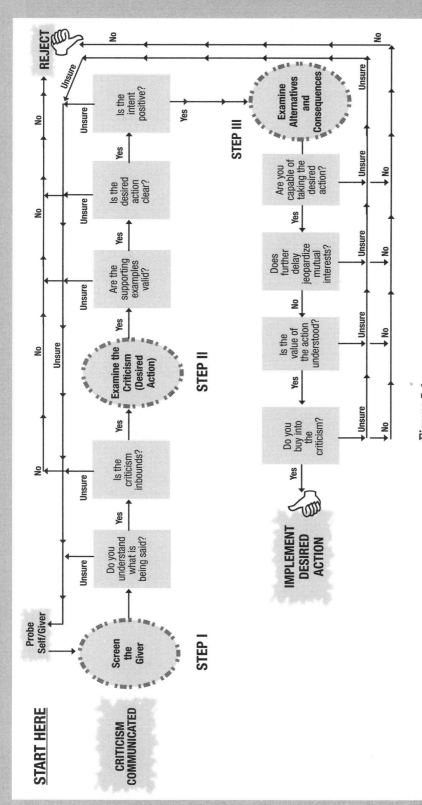

Figure 5-1.
THE RECEIVER CONTROL CHART

OVERVIEW OF THE THREE STEPS NECESSARY IN RECEIVING CRITICISM

The Receiver Control Chart is divided into three steps. Each step is designed to coincide with how you naturally would assess criticism coming your way.

STEP I:
Screen the Giver

Step I focuses on your initial thoughts of "who is this person and will I accept criticism from him?"

STEP II:
Examine the Criticism (Desired Action)

Step II shifts the focus to the criticism itself. Through a series of questions, it helps you to assess whether or not productive value can be gained from the criticism.

STEP III:
Examine Alternatives and Consequences

Step III takes your emotions into account. Questions raised in this step are designed to help you examine how you feel about the criticism, whether or not you are willing and able to take action, and what consequences are potentially involved if you delay or reject the criticism.

Just as the giver needs to learn to think before speaking, the receiver of criticism needs to inspect what's being said before reacting. With this in mind, let's analyze the process of handling criticism once it is delivered. As each of the steps is introduced, keep in mind that when there is uncertainty, the Receiver Control Chart directs you to probe yourself as well as the giver. This translates to asking questions at any time during or after the conversation. You may prefer to think about what's been said before responding. The validity of this preference is reflected in the Receiver Control Chart. As mentioned previously, there may be many rounds with criticism. No need to panic! Having to say something right then and there is rarely if ever required. Likewise, formulating all your questions on the spot in most cases is not necessary. You can always come back at another time to gain a greater understanding of the situation. If you elect to remain silent during the real-time criticism exchange, you may want to state at an appropriate point that you may return to the conversation in the future, so the person criticizing you doesn't misinterpret your desire not to say anything as disinterest, resistance, or orneriness on your part.

COACHING TIP #13:

Insight into Keeping an Open Mind

Keeping an open mind is an important mental step that requires a proper set of attitudes. Just how important is that attitude set? Try this quick exercise. Read through the following questions and answer them honestly:

► Do you think you can gain *some* benefit from criticism?

► Do you *strongly* believe that you can benefit from criticism?

If you answered "yes" to these two questions, then it would be accurate to conclude that you have a positive attitude toward criticism. Here's your final question:

► Will you readily accept criticism from someone you do not respect?

If you are like the thousands of people who have been asked this question, the unequivocal answer is "no."

This quick yet insightful exercise makes two terrific points. First, it demonstrates how quickly and easily our behaviors become out of sync with our attitude. After all, you said that you are receptive to criticism—but only so far! Second, it's important that you be made aware that there is a natural tendency to immediately reject what someone you don't respect has to say. More specifically, you want to utilize the control that's yours to get past who is delivering the criticism and listen with an open mind to what's being said in order to determine if there's any benefit to be gained from the criticism.

Finally, even though you can reject what's being said at any time, it's best to mentally run through the entire Receiver Control Chart before rejecting the criticism. Why? Because you need to have each of the steps embedded in your mind so that when you encounter criticism from a questionable giver and are feeling uneasy, you can accurately and quickly sift through what's being said and factor in what's happening at the moment. This is in contrast to fumbling under the pressure because you haven't fine-tuned your listening and receiving skills. The choice is yours.

THE THREE STEPS

STEP I:
Screen the Giver

Zeroing in on who is delivering the criticism is a natural response that can instantly color what is being said, so it's essential to stay open-minded. Imagine a laser beam, and position it to go beyond "who" the person is, including his status, tone of voice, choice of words, posture, and so on. Instead, position the beam so your attention is directed at the "what" as you consider the questions shown in Figure 5-2.

Figure 5-2.
STEP I OF THE RECEIVER CONTROL CHART

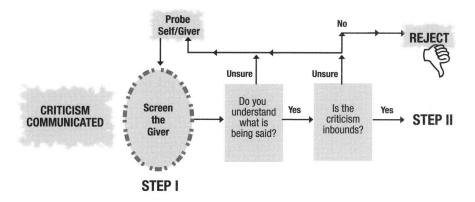

Step I, Question 1: *Do You Understand What Is Being Said?*

Before getting to the criticism itself, we need to touch on a few important considerations. As an example, your willingness to hear "what" is being said depends on your past experience with the giver and the quality of your relationship. If you are intimidated, don't like the giver, or mistrust him, then chances are great that you will ignore what is being said. Also, if the person has given you lousy advice in the past or is a known enemy, the tendency is to immediately disregard what he has to say. You may also quickly jump to conclusions that what's being said is an unfair attack when it's not, and you will respond defensively. In each of these situations, you would be making a mistake.

Another consideration to watch out for where we often run into trouble is quickly viewing neutral facts as implied criticisms. Think about the boss who tells you your expense report is a week late or a peer who points out that you haven't dropped off the book you promised. In each case, if you interpret the facts as implied criticisms and respond defensively, givers can come back and say something along the lines of: "It's difficult to have a conversation with you because you become so defensive. All I was trying to do was make the point that you are past due with the expense report," or "I was just trying to remind you that you forgot the book." You can fall into the same embarrassing trap if you make the leap and view opinions or perceptions as implied criticisms.

After running into these givers a couple of times, you want to use your control and say, "Thanks for making me aware"—and nothing more. If you are unsure, you can probe the giver as the Receiver Control Chart recommends and ask, "Is this just for my information and nothing more?" Granted, avoiding the tendency to respond defensively may be hard when you are dealing with someone who you feel doesn't have your best interest in mind. But once again, you have the control and it's up to you to use it. Don't give givers such authority over you that they are able to truly shake you up!

Focus on the "What" and Ask Questions When Unsure As you focus on the "what," you need to ask yourself: "Do I understand the criticism?" For example, during a performance review, would you understand what your boss means when she says, "You are too perfect"? Would you understand when she casually says, "It's important that you contribute more at meetings"? Would you be able to interpret correctly if a colleague says, "You need to pay more attention to relationships and not get so wrapped up in the success of the project"? If you take such comments as criticisms, then what is the real meaning behind these criticisms? If you are unsure, the process guides you to probe. Other than yourself, in each example, the best person to probe is the giver.

One of the examples mentioned above was the critical comment "You are too perfect." Let's say an employee received that comment during her performance review. After deliberating for a while, she decides to go back to her boss to find out what he meant. Lo and behold, he tells her that she is an excellent performer, but she doesn't stretch herself. She only takes on assignments that she knows she can do extremely well. He wants her to take some risks and move into areas that are less familiar and would offer her a great opportunity to learn new skills. You may be as surprised as the employee is when her boss provides that detailed explanation. What's important here is to use your control as the receiver to make sure you clearly understand the criticism.

COACHING TIP #14:

Dealing with the "Who"

Here's a quick exercise to help you gain personal insight when dealing with persons giving you criticism:

- ► Think of someone you respect and have an easy time accepting criticism from. Determine what makes it easy to accept criticism from her, and make a mental note or write it down.

- ► Think of someone you have a more difficult time accepting criticism from. What makes it difficult? Again, make a mental note or write it down.

Looking at these two extremes will give you some valuable insights about yourself as a receiver and will help you pinpoint more accurately where you want to exert control.

Here's another valuable insight. Chances are great that when you were selecting someone who was "difficult," you picked an individual who falls into your "enemy camp" category. Well, it's valuable to remind yourself of the old adage "Keep your friends close and your enemies closer." This expression is so applicable to criticism because while your friends may not always tell you the truth for fear of jeopardizing the friendship, your enemy couldn't care less. While you may often consider your enemy's purpose to be destructive and hurtful, remember that you have the control. So rather than immediately turn off and not listen, do the opposite. Listen carefully and weed through what he is saying, layer by layer, like an onion, because in the end, there may be a grain of truth! After all, your enemy has nothing to lose in telling you.

Step I, Question 2: *Is the Criticism Inbounds?*

This question touches on two important areas: who is saying it and that person's relationship to the content and timing.

Content What you look for regarding content is whether the criticism falls within the expectations and roles established in the relationship. Let's say your boss mentioned during a casual conversation that you are spending too much time at work and are neglecting loved ones at home. While you and your boss may have a good relationship, you might reject the criticism, feeling that she has overstepped her bounds. After all, what you do with your personal time is up to you. However, if your doctor told you that you were working too many hours and needed to spend more time relaxing and being with your family, you might have a different reaction to the "criticism." In fact, you would even consider it advice rather than criticism. Likewise, say a peer criticized you after the two of you met with a customer, commenting that the way you responded to the customer's questions was troublesome. You might reject the criticism because your peer is not your boss, and furthermore, he doesn't know what went on between you and the customer prior to the meeting. "Who" delivers the criticism plays a significant part in whether or not the criticism is considered inbounds. But, once again, zero in on the content and the intent of the message and, in many cases, don't be so intent on labeling what could be intended as advice as criticism.

If you are unsure about whether the criticism is inbounds, then it's best to check out the intent behind it with the person who delivered the criticism. Find out what her purpose is and why she felt compelled to say something.

If you believe givers are out of bounds, it's best to share your objections, expectations, or preferences with them—especially those with whom you interact frequently. That way, you further develop a mutual understanding or a Matched Relationship Expectation Package. Having this kind of conversation with your boss may prove especially worthwhile.

Timing Timing is quite often related to appropriateness and receptivity. Having your boss, for example, point out an error typically may not ignite your emotional fuse and cause you to take issue with the criticism. But if your boss catches you at a bad time, chances become more likely that this is exactly what you will do. At these times, you are vulnerable and not a receptive receiver. This is when you kindly warn others to tread lightly. One food and beverage manager warned her staff and brought a little humor along the way when she posted a message on her office door that read: "I'm 49% bitch today, so don't push it."

Sometimes you don't know until it's too late. It's as if the criticism served as the match to set off an emotional reaction that you didn't even know was building up inside you. When these unfortunate situations occur (and they do because we are all human), that's when you and the person delivering the criticism can hopefully dip into the quality of your relationship and show some understanding, flexibility, and forgiveness. If the relationship is weak, then you have some repair work to do. In either case, it's important to be timely about getting back to the person who delivered the criticism to apologize for how you reacted. Whether the person forgives you or not is in his control—but at least you took initiative to try to mend the relationship. Remember, there are many rounds of criticism, so be patient as well as understanding. Remind yourself your job is to work with the person. It's not necessary to like him. That perspective goes both ways.

STEP II:

Examine the Criticism

This is the most crucial of all the steps shown in the Receiver Control Chart. You've now gotten past who is delivering the criticism, and you've considered whether you understand the criticism and whether it's inbounds. In this step—shown in Figure 5-3—you are continuing to listen for specific examples, and it is at this point where you begin thinking of what to do to correct the situation. Simultaneously, you're looking for all kinds of clues about the giver's intent. These are the topic areas that are raised as questions in Step II.

Figure 5-3.
STEP II OF THE RECEIVER CONTROL CHART

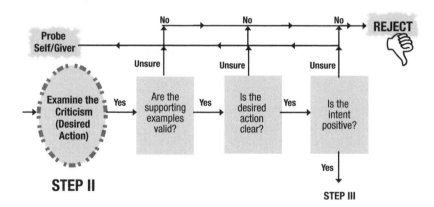

Step II, Question 3: *Are the Supporting Examples Valid?*

One of the ways to determine if the criticism is acceptable is to look for specific examples that are accurate. Furthermore, check to see whether the specific examples used support the criticism.

Here's a terrific scenario that illustrates how one manager inspected the validity of the examples used during a criticism exchange with his boss. Juan works as the director of training for a large computer company. During his last performance review, Juan's boss, Michael, pointed out that Juan needed to be more organized. Michael offered a few substantial examples to illustrate Juan's lack of organizational skills.

Let's fast-forward three months. Since the performance review, the company has been through a downsizing. Everyone, including Juan, has been forced to take on additional responsibilities. One new assignment given to Juan that's very visible within the company is overseeing a three-day global technical conference for senior executives. In preparation for the meeting, Juan and his team needed to collect technical papers from each of the twenty presenters, who were senior managers. Juan had received all but six of the papers. Until they received these last six papers, Juan and his team could not move forward to produce the hard-copy workbooks and accompanying CDs necessary for all of the attendees.

Juan and his team were starting to panic because the conference was only three days away. Feeling pressured, Juan sent out a carefully worded personal email requesting that the six senior managers turn in their papers right away. Three came in, which left Juan with three papers outstanding. He decided to follow up with a phone call to each of the remaining senior managers, knowing that how he approached them would be very important because he was much lower in rank. One by one, the final papers came in. Finally, by 3 p.m. on Friday afternoon, in a nail-biting effort, Juan and his team scurried around at lightning speed to proof and compile the papers before producing the workbooks and CDs. This was the last thing that needed to be done for the conference, which was scheduled to start at 8 a.m. the next morning.

Saturday morning came, and most of the 350 senior executives who had registered showed up. Juan's boss, who was nervous at the outset, soon began to relax as he saw that everything was running smoothly. The conference was a great success.

On Tuesday morning, Michael stopped by Juan's office to tell him what a terrific job he and his team had done to pull the event off as well as they did. But before Juan could say "thank you," Michael followed up his praise by saying, "As I said, you all did a great job, but on

Friday, everyone was running around doing last-minute things. If I'm not mistaken, you didn't leave the office until 8:30 that night. You know, if you were a little more organized, as we discussed during your performance review a few months ago, you and your team wouldn't have had to do all that last-minute hustling!"

Upon hearing this, Juan was quick to reject Michael's criticism because he knew that Michael's example wasn't accurate. He stopped listening and stopped making eye contact. Juan said nothing, repositioning his body as if to signal that he was ready to end this conversation and resume his work. Saying nothing was probably a smart decision on Juan's part because he was known for being passionate about his work and on occasion would react emotionally. On the other hand, Juan's immediate rejection of the criticism shut him off from possibly learning something of value. He also would have been better off keeping an open mind and running through all of the steps to receiving quality criticism, because doing so would help him to continue to fine-tune his listening skills and his ability to inspect information more accurately. Besides, demonstrating receptivity to what Michael had to say shows respect. As it was, Michael left Juan's office thinking that Juan was resistant to his comments. The good thing is that Juan never lost control, even though he thought he was wronged. In addition, because criticism can have many rounds, Juan is in the position to take some time to consider the entire exchange with Michael in its full context and come back later to set the record straight and smooth things out with his boss.

Step II, Question 4: *Is the Desired Action Clear?*

While you may place importance on having specific examples to validate a criticism, knowing the specific desired action to take will prove in the end to be of greatest importance. As you learned in Chapter 2, one of the biggest mistakes receivers make is assuming that the corrective action is implicitly spelled out in the criticism. If emphasis isn't placed on knowing specifically what to do, receivers end up guessing. You know what that means if you guess incorrectly: More criticisms will probably result.

An important caveat comes with knowing the specific desired action to take from the giver's perspective. What do you do if the person delivering the criticism doesn't offer or know the desired action? What if he says something along the lines of: "I pay you too much money—you figure it out!"? Don't despair. You have the control, so use it to figure out what you need to do to correct the situation. Then be sure to pass your ideas by the person giving the criticism to make sure he is in agreement and believes you are directing your energies wisely. The important thing here is that you are not a victim in this type of situation.

Step II, Question 5: *Is the Intent Positive?*

When being criticized, it's natural to ask yourself: "Is this criticism intended to place blame on me? To embarrass me? To hurt me? To destroy me? Or is it meant to help me?"

Sorting out the intention behind the criticism isn't easy. During workshop discussions, my company surveyed hundreds of people regarding how they determine the giver's intent. Many said they use plain old intuition. One Chicago doctor captured it best when he said, "I can't always put my finger on exactly how I know when someone's intention is constructive or not. But I can sense it and my experience has shown me that I am almost always correct in my feelings." If your intuition is developed, it is probably your most reliable tool in assessing another person's intentions.

When we questioned people further on this, some clues were mentioned quite regularly. These clues, which are worth noting here, send an immediate signal to you that the giver's intent may not be positive:

- ► The giver fails to look you in the eye (especially if the giver generally looks you in the eye during a regular conversation).

- ► The giver exaggerates the criticism.

- ► The giver compares you with an identified, known enemy.

► The giver talks in generalities.

► The examples offered do not align with the criticism.

► The giver offers no corrective action.

► It remains unclear who will benefit from the criticism.

► The giver approaches you at a time or place where you are likely to be upset by the criticism.

► After being informed of your sensitivity to certain words or phrases, the giver deliberately uses them.

► The giver is quick to cut off your response.

If one or more of these clues are present, alarms should go off in your head. The clear message is that you need to immediately start questioning the giver's intent. If you are unsure, the Receiver Control Chart directs you to probe the giver. In asking questions of the giver, you are clarifying what is not being said.

A good way to ask for clarification is to say, "How do you want me to take this?" or "Help me understand how this is trying to be helpful." During a meeting, you could ask, "Moving forward, how should I interpret this?" A bolder, more direct question is: "I'm not sure . . . what's your purpose right now?"

When probing the giver under these circumstances, it is extremely important to be aware of your tone of voice. A challenging tone could easily add fuel to the fire! Keep your purpose clearly in the forefront of your mind. Stay open-minded and listen carefully.

There are times when colleagues say something that's clearly what I refer to as "down the middle," and you're not sure what to make of what they said. For instance, during a casual conversation with a group of peers after work, someone laughingly blurts out, "Yeah, for a little person [the employee is 5 feet tall], you pack quite a punch when trying to influence others." Or you turn in a report and a coworker remarks, "Well, this looks okay for someone who whipped this report out really fast!" Or after you present an idea in a meeting, someone at the table says, "That's an interesting idea." In each of these situations, you can ignore what was said. After all, you are in control. You can also respond defensively and run the risk of having others come back and accuse you of not having a sense of humor or of being too sensitive and misinterpreting the message. The best way to exercise control—especially for the giver who says "That's an interesting idea"—is to follow the process and probe the giver by responding, "What did you find most interesting about the idea?" That way, you reveal the giver's vagueness or true intent. A favorite question I've memorized that works extremely well on the fly when someone says "That's interesting" is to ask the following: "Is that 'interesting' meant to be a good interesting, or a bad interesting? How do you want me to take this?" If you are not satisfied with the response and feel that the giver's intent isn't to be helpful, you can consider other courses of action, including ignoring the presumed criticism altogether.

Even though not all givers mean to be helpful, it's still reasonable to operate from a premise of positive intent, where the criticism is intended to have a constructive end result and the individual criticizing you is doing so in good faith. Take another look at the clues that cause alarm bells to go off, and you may conclude that what's really going on is that the giver is unskilled at giving criticism. Use your control to take enough time to consider what's going on at that very moment as you silently work through the entire Receiver Control Chart. While mentally going through the process, consider this perspective: It would be much more harmful for the giver not to criticize and let you continue doing what he believed to be incorrect! Sorting out the intention is a good way for you to exercise control. However, if you conclude that a giver's intention is to hurt you, then you are in control of rejecting the criticism. What may be going on is that you have a real problem in the relationship that goes beyond any one criticism. It's up to you if you want to make attempts to mend the relationship or not.

STEP III:
Examine Alternatives and Consequences

To be able to sort through the giver's intent and logically inspect the criticism, you must keep your emotions in check. Step III of the Receiver Control Chart, shown in Figure 5-4, helps you to work with your emotions and sort out what is happening in the larger picture.

Figure 5-4.
STEP III OF THE RECEIVER CONTROL CHART

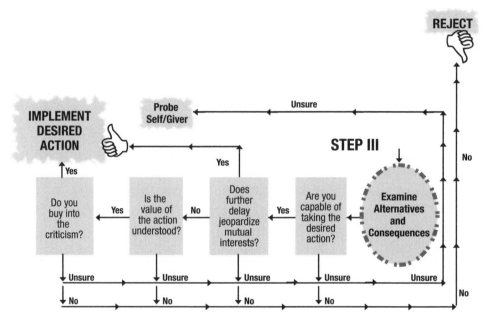

Experience has taught you that asking questions and trying to engage in a conversation with the giver on the spot is *not* always the most effective thing to do. Just because you are on the receiving end of criticism doesn't mean you have to respond. You have the control and so you may determine it's best to remain silent with certain givers.

Using your energies to consider the broader circumstances surrounding the criticism, which includes assessing emotional levels for all parties involved, helps you determine how best to respond. You truly are not compelled to respond specifically to the criticism, nor can you be forced to say anything after being criticized. When emotions are stirred up and overflowing, it's often difficult to stay focused. In these circumstances, what often happens is that you end up saying things that may win the battle but lose the war!

Depending on who is giving the criticism and what he is saying, it may be best simply to accept what is said at the moment, rather than try to "set the record straight" or "have your turn to speak." Knowing how best to handle yourself in certain situations hinges on your ability to accurately pick up on clues of all kinds, be they visual or auditory. Asking yourself some key questions can help you interpret what is going on during a criticism exchange and can sharpen your sensitivities to the situation.

Step III, Question 6: *Are You Capable of Taking the Desired Action?*

Receivers often fail to consider this key question. Even if the giver's intention is to be helpful, as the receiver, it's of utmost importance that you allow your emotions to settle long enough to put the situation in perspective and consider if you are capable of and willing to make the corrective measures being asked of you. Failing to consider this question only leads to further complications down the road. Remember, what's implied with criticism is change. Associated with that change are real or imagined consequences.

Exercise your control to determine if the changes being asked of you are the kind of changes you want to make or are capable of making. Take for example Kyle, a young, ambitious, overly confident engineer who offered to write a technical paper for his team's most recent project. After all, when he was in school, everyone told him he was a good writer. Reality set in when the project head—who had twenty-three years of experience and had published numerous papers of his own—criticized Kyle's paper. The criticisms he offered were specific, and there were many. When stepping back and taking some time to assess the situation, Kyle realized he was over his head. Rather than give up, he came back to the project head and humbly asked for help.

Sometimes when you step back and put the criticism in perspective, you discover that it was based on your being new in your role. This was the case with Sally, who recently started working as the administrative assistant for Dave, a midsize company's vice president of sales. Dave flies extensively, and he was very upset with Sally when she booked a flight at the wrong time. Feeling terrible about the situation, Sally retraced in her mind what led up to the mistake. She concluded that she was new and simply was not aware of the fact that Dave insisted on never taking the last flight of the night when he needed to be at a destination the next morning. She apologized profusely to Dave for the error and assured him that she would do better next time. She also went on to say it wasn't a matter of incompetence or lack of desire to do a good job—it was simply the result of her being new. Interestingly, Dave appreciated what Sally communicated, because he too had forgotten that she was new to the job. After all, things were going so smoothly that he had lost that perspective.

As these examples illustrate, you need to assess whether you are capable of and want to take action. Thinking this through may require more time than is available right then, as in the case with Kyle. An option is to request a recess: Ask the giver if you can get back to the conversation at a later time. If you are unsure about your capability, you can always probe the giver and ask what makes her believe that you can make the change. After all, sometimes we are not aware of our potential. Others can see what we can't, and it's then that you need to place your trust in others.

Step III, Question 7: *Does Further Delay Jeopardize Mutual Interests?*

When you are dealing with real-time criticism, you need to quickly assess the big picture or broader perspective. Be sure to include in your assessment emotional levels and who is present. Specifically, you need to consider what is at stake if you probe or resist the giver. What is at risk if you resist taking any action at all? In making this judgment, you need to instantly factor in the urgency of the moment, everything you know about the giver, all spoken and unspoken expectations, the intensity of the giver's delivery, and your observations of the situation at hand as well as prior situations. All this is silently racing through your mind, as it did for Stacey. She had recently started working at a high-end women's dress shop in Manhattan where she experienced the following situation.

While helping a regular customer select a leisure wardrobe for her upcoming cruise, Stacey pulled some outfits off the rack that were the wrong size and style. The manager quickly stepped in and said to Stacey in front of the customer, "These are the wrong size and style. Go downstairs where we have her size. There's a leisure suit on rack five that I want you to bring up." Stacey was momentarily taken aback by the manager's curt and aggressive approach. She tried to process what had happened. A number of conflicting thoughts went through her mind, including the embarrassment she felt at the moment for having been criticized in front of the customer. Her emotions were further shaken because she was offended by her boss's abrupt and forceful approach. While factoring in all this, she also took a big-picture view and sensed the urgency of the situation. She decided to say nothing more than "Fine," as she left the floor to retrieve the clothes. If Stacey had resisted and challenged her boss, she might have achieved what's called a Pyrrhic victory, winning the battle and losing the war.

Timing, which is ever important, includes where you are emotionally at a given moment. For instance, what might have happened if Stacey was in a terrible mood or wasn't feeling well? We will never know. What we do know is that Stacey hesitated. Perhaps during that brief second of hesitation, she recognized that as the receiver, she had the control at that moment. Because she had the control, she could always revisit the situation later, when the timing was better and everyone's emotions were calmer. Keep in mind that we are talking about an art form, not a science that yields consistent, predetermined outcomes. By learning how to utilize the control that is inherently yours, you get the opportunity to make a choice as opposed to responding in a reactionary way where you feel you have no options.

Step III, Question 8: *Is the Value of the Action Understood?*

It's not enough to know what you did wrong and what you need to do moving forward. You want to know what value is to be gained by taking the corrective action. There is only a slim likelihood that you will make a lasting change in your behavior if you see no value in the change. In other words, adults don't invest time and energy to bring about sustained changes in their behavior just because they are told to do so. At first you may comply, especially if the criticism is coming from your boss, because you want to keep your job. But over time, you will most likely revert back to your old habits if you don't understand or experience what value is to be gained. If the giver lets the criticism exchange go by without telling *why* it is important to make the changes, and if you don't see the importance yourself, then you owe it to yourself and the giver to find out. As the process suggests, ask the giver to help you understand why making certain changes is beneficial.

If you forgot to ask, think on your own about whether you perceive the value to be gained as valid and meaningful. If you are still having difficulty determining why taking the action is necessary, go back at a later time to probe the giver, rather than elect to reject the criticism outright.

Here's an example that illustrates how misperceptions arise when receivers don't exercise their control to find out the value to be gained by criticism. It's often only in hindsight that the benefit becomes apparent. To set the stage, imagine you are a fly on the wall listening to a group of seasoned managers enjoying themselves at their local hangout after work. The conversation is about their former boss, Ben. Everyone at the table had previously worked for him at one point in their career. Ben was a tough, detailed, no-nonsense type who placed tremendous demands on his managers. They all laugh as they recall specific times when Ben would rip them up and down with criticisms for not having their financials perfect, for not being able to adequately answer challenging questions, or for errors in their PowerPoint slides. No one escaped Ben's wrath. With laughter still in the air, they collectively decide to anoint themselves as disciples of "Ben's University."

The laughter dies down when one manager bravely admits to how frustrated and confused he felt back then. He confesses that he didn't know where he stood with Ben. Often, his confidence would be badly shaken. In order to survive, he told himself that Ben was just a mean boss whom he had to endure because he had to keep his job in order to put food on the table. Others at the table chime in and agree. Then another manager takes the stage and reminds the group of how one man had asked to be transferred out of Ben's group because he didn't like Ben's abusive management style. "While that's all true," says another manager, "let's not forget our first experiences presenting to senior management! They were brutally tough. Because of Ben, though, we were prepared and did a good job." Everyone starts to laugh again, as no one denies the value they had gained from all of Ben's criticisms.

What's unfortunate about this scene is that Ben never explained the value to be gained from his being so demanding and tough. There's no denying that point. All well and good, but the managers also could have avoided all the anguish and frustration they had felt if they had only exercised their control by questioning Ben to better understand his purpose and the value to be gained by his tough criticisms.

So, regardless of whether you object to how some criticism is presented, if you see some value in what the giver is pointing out, then you need to look at the bigger picture, check your emotions, and ask yourself why it isn't the wise thing to just buy into the criticism.

Step III, Question 9: *Do You Buy Into the Criticism?*

This last question gives you an opportunity to step back and view the situation from afar to check out your overall thoughts and feelings. It's important to consider the criticism even though you can reject it at any point in the conversation. Some of us can process information very quickly. If that describes you, then you want to review what was said and ask yourself if you clearly know what you are to do to address the situation. Also, ask if you know the potential value to be gained. If at any point you aren't clear about what specific actions you need to take or why it's important to take them, it's hard to accurately determine if you buy into the criticism. Likewise, if your tendency is to focus more on "how" the criticism is delivered, which means that you possibly miss what's been said, you too may find it difficult to accurately assess whether you buy into the criticism. Reflecting on the criticism gives you an opportunity to evaluate the giver's intent, the situation surrounding the criticism, and how credible the criticism is. Some of us may require additional time to sort all this out.

Likewise, if you are in a bad mood at the time or have a tendency to respond emotionally to any criticism, then you might find it helpful to "sleep on it" because things may look different in the light of the next morning. Always remind yourself that as a receiver, you are in control, and exercising that control may require some extra time to let things settle. Experience has taught you that snapping back too quickly has not served you well either at work or at home. So taking some extra time before responding may be exactly what you want to do. It's giving yourself permission to take your own "adult time-out" to assess what you've just heard so you avoid speaking too soon and regretting it later.

Then again, because the control ultimately lies with you, getting emotional may be exactly what you want to do. Perhaps you're tired of dealing with the same issue and not getting anywhere, and you need to let others know how strongly you feel. What's different here is that you are making a conscious decision to express how you feel as opposed to flying off the handle because you are out of control.

As you consider each situation, the Receiver Control Chart should be used to help you inspect the criticism you receive and position yourself to benefit as the receiver. Once again, what we are talking about isn't a science. It's an art form!

Quick Review for Easy Recall

The Receiver Control Chart is a mental process for keeping you open-minded as you view what's being said as merely information. When inspecting the information, ask the following questions to exercise your control:

Step I: Screen the giver.

    1. Do you understand what is being said?

    2. Is the criticism inbounds?

Step II: Examine the criticism.

    3. Are the supporting examples valid?

    4. Is the desired action clear?

    5. Is the intent positive?

Step III: Examine alternatives and consequences.

    6. Are you capable of taking the desired action?

    7. Does further delay jeopardize mutual interests?

    8. Is the value of the action understood?

    9. Do you buy into the criticism?

If the answer to every question on the checklist is "yes," move on to the next step: Take action. If the answer to any question is "no," reject the criticism. If you are unsure of any of the answers, ask more questions of yourself and the giver.

CHAPTER 6

Avoiding the Tendency to Personalize Criticism

> *He only profits from praise who values criticism.*
>
> —ATTRIBUTED TO HEINRICH HEINE

Amerca's longest serving First Lady was Eleanor Roosevelt, a woman who suffered many indignities and insults over her long and fascinating life. Her parents ridiculed her as an unattractive child, and her husband, President Franklin Roosevelt, carried on affairs that were an open secret. Yet she emerged as a proud and poised woman to all who came in contact with her. This was a person who clearly understood the stinging wounds of criticism. Nevertheless, she came up with the ultimate statement of strength in the face of harsh commentary when she said, "No one can make you feel inferior without your consent."[1] In this all-important chapter, that belief will guide us forward. You will learn how to manage the emotional dynamics of criticism so that you do not take it personally and, at the same time, take the control that is justly in your hands. So often when we first hear criticism, our sensitivities are bruised, our emotions get churned up, and we wind up feeling that we are personally being berated. Minimizing such initial reactions becomes important in order to keep our composure and truly listen to what is being said.

To set the framework, you will be introduced to three proven de-emotionalizing skills for doing this. Deploy these skills and you'll be able to permanently remove the annoying stress and sleepless nights caused by criticism from others. The chapter also includes a look at how to avoid responding defensively to criticism.

The three de-emotionalizing skills delivered beneficial outcomes to the hundreds of participants who engaged in the Strategies for Enhancing Performance Study. Findings revealed a significant difference between experimental group participants and the control group in the ability to benefit when placed on the receiving end of criticism. Having these skills in your tool kit is important. We all need to be properly equipped to objectively interpret what is happening at the moment we find ourselves receiving criticism.

Generally speaking, no one starts his day looking forward to being criticized. When someone finds fault with us, we usually feel anxiety. In fact, survey respondents from the Strategies for Enhancing Performance Study rated being on the receiving end of criticism as the second most stressful situation encountered at work. This chapter will help you deal with that stress and anxiety.

TAKING THE STING OUT OF CRITICISM

To get started, let's look at some questions about how you react when criticized:

- ► Do you tend to automatically assume that the person criticizing you is correct?

- ► Do your emotions become stirred when someone is criticizing you?

- ► Do you quickly become defensive?

- ► Do you stop listening while the criticism is being delivered?

► Do you take criticism personally?

► While the criticism is delivered, do you sometimes think your image in the eyes of the giver is destroyed?

There are no right or wrong answers here. What's important is being aware of how you typically respond to criticism and whether or not your responses position you to learn something of value and strengthen your relationships with others. Let's examine how Yana, a young, high-potential manager, responded to a disastrous situation. For the past three years, Yana has reported to Liz, one of the company's few female executives. Liz wouldn't hesitate to tell others that getting to the top wasn't easy. Since Liz sees great potential in Yana, she demands a lot from her and gives her many responsibilities. Even with two children at home, Yana doesn't mind all the long hours because she's eager to advance. Besides, with everything that Liz has asked her to do, Yana has made great contacts in the company and learned quickly.

Among the many duties Yana finds on her to-do list is setting up an off-site afternoon conference involving all of Liz's peers, who represent the company's technical disciplines. Planning the event includes juggling lots of logistics. One of the more cumbersome tasks that Liz has assigned to Yana is arranging a survey-taking system for the conference.

Because Liz's upper-level peers will be in attendance, Yana takes special precautions in advance to make sure everything will run perfectly. The day of the event, she is still checking and double-checking. She is in constant contact with the banquet manager at the hotel where the conference is being held to ensure that all details have been properly handled. Prior to leaving for the hotel, Yana and her team tested the company's cordless poll-taking devices, which will be used in taking the survey during the conference. Yana even arranged to bring the company's in-house technician with her in case anything went wrong at the event. Once at the hotel, the team tests the equipment one more time. Everything is working as expected, and all preparations for the event are completed.

With a sigh of relief, Yana welcomes the managers as they start pouring into the large conference room. The event kicks off with Liz delivering an inspiring message about how best to open up new markets. Just as she is about to finish, she asks the managers to cast their votes about whether or not they are in favor of introducing two new products mentioned during her presentation. It's time for the poll-taking devices to operate. Even though they had worked successfully an hour before, they now fail to operate. Panic strikes as Liz looks visibly upset at Yana. Yana and the technician frantically try to sort out what could have gone wrong as everyone waits patiently. Nothing. The devices are still not working. Liz tries to recover, but she is so infuriated that all she can say is, "Let's take a ten-minute break."

As everyone leaves the room to partake in the excellent array of refreshments and treats that Yana arranged, Liz walks over to Yana and the technician to get a better handle on what's happening. Stressed out and exhausted, Yana and the technician report that they have no idea what went wrong. Giving it one last try, they finally get the equipment to work. The technician has no idea what he did to get the system to operate successfully. Everyone returns to the meeting room, and the event unfolds smoothly.

In the meantime, the technical difficulties have taken their toll on Yana. The final blow is when Liz says to her during the next break, "How could you let me down? Why didn't you better prepare for such an event?" Yana can't hold back her tears and is devastated. Forget about sleeping that night. She lies awake as she keeps replaying the day's events in her mind. For several weeks following the event, Yana's confidence is rattled. She lacks her typical enthusiasm and drive to make things happen. Her beautiful smile, long such a welcome sight around the office, is scarcely seen.

Most of us have been through a similar ordeal at one time or another. We're painfully aware that being on the receiving end of criticism can be tough. Very few of us have learned how to effectively guide ourselves along and successfully control our emotions when criticism hits hard. As participants in the Strategies for Enhancing Performance Study learned, handling criticism well is a skill that requires practice, not so different from the process of learning a new software program. It takes patience, insight, and a willingness to explore what is really going on. And yet the experimental group in the study, as previously mentioned, did learn to deploy procedures that resulted in a significant improvement in their effectiveness at handling criticism when compared to their colleagues who did not receive the training.[2] You're about to learn these skills.

To set the framework, be aware that our research has shown that how and why people "personalize criticism" varies and is based on each individual's experiences. For many, a common reaction following the exchange is hurt and resentment. It's possible for the pain to continue for days and even weeks. Stop and think about what's really going on when someone is hurt by criticism. Certainly, you've heard the expression "The truth hurts." And we have come to believe that people sometimes need to feel hurt before they are motivated to change behavior.

However, we found in our research that for most of us, "personalizing the criticism" involves an immediate emotional reaction that sometimes impairs clear thinking and the ability to engage in a meaningful exchange. If this begins to describe how you react, then you need to know that you can take some specific actions to de-emotionalize the exchange. Remember, *as the receiver you are in control*, and it's important that you use this control effectively. The participants in the Strategies for Enhancing Performance Study came out of their four-hour training program having learned specific techniques and insights. One of the most effective ways to take control is to learn *quick charges*, which are easily self-adjusting, neatly packaged techniques used instantly in situations to help you regain control and direct your energies more productively. Quick charges are your secret weapons for retaining emotional control of situations as they occur. There's no trick to using these de-emotionalizing techniques effectively; it just takes a commitment to use them and a little practice. Don't worry too much about having opportunities to practice because everyday experiences at work and home will provide them for you! Let's explore what goes into learning the skill of de-emotionalizing criticism. To de-emotionalize criticism so that it does not get interpreted as a personal attack, it is essential to pay attention to the following:

1. Your personal self-confidence

2. The need to maintain a big-picture focus

3. Inspecting what others say

DE-EMOTIONALIZING CRITICISM:
THE SELF-CONFIDENCE FACTOR

Before we get into the specific quick charges you can use in de-emotionalizing criticism, it is important to discuss what is at the root of exercising control in the handling of criticism. That root factor is self-confidence, or the faith we have in our abilities, skills, and potential for success. It's when we tell ourselves: "I know from past experience that I have what it takes to complete a particular task or goal." As one manager succinctly said, "Confidence is the feeling you have before getting all the facts." Confidence, however, is like the weather because it fluctuates from one day to the next. Obviously, criticism is easier to handle when your confidence level is high compared to when it is low. Criticism can pull the self-confidence rug right out from under us if we let it. Some people use criticism to do just that. We have to be aware and explore the motivation of others who give us criticism before we let it penetrate our level of confidence.

When confidence levels are high, it's easier to listen to what the giver has to say without immediately letting the words pierce through. We can more easily and accurately sift through what's being said. An excellent example of someone who exudes self-confidence is Tim Tebow, Heisman Trophy winner and former NFL quarterback. Ever since he came on the grand stage, he's been criticized for his religious practices and his failures to play up to expectations. His previous teammates on the New York Jets even ripped him behind his back to the press. With all of the criticism hurled at him, Tebow responded to ESPN reporters, saying, "It's never fun to hear criticism, but at the same time, it's something I've always used as motivation, and you try to get stronger from it."[3]

What do you do if your confidence is low? Can you do something to boost it? The answer is yes—we can learn to become more confident. How?

One of my diving coaches forced me to think about this question years ago. After a frustrating workout in West Palm Beach, Florida, I emerged from the pool with tears in my eyes. My coach came over and put her arms around me and whispered in my ear, "Debbie, you can be a champion. Everything is there—all you need to do is believe in yourself and be more confident." I immediately thought to myself, "That's easy for you to say, but hard for me to do."

Nevertheless, shortly after her words sunk in, I got goose bumps and thought, "Wait a minute! Somebody believes in me." That's great, but at the same time, I wondered with a lump in my throat how I could become confident. After years of asking myself and others this question, I've discovered some sure ways to build self-confidence.

Here's a quick yet powerful way to unveil what goes into building self-confidence. Think and ask yourself, "What are my strengths?" Then list them. When reviewing your list, ask yourself how you know these are your strengths. Perhaps you have based your list on what people have told you, on your own experiences, or on the results you've achieved. By considering what you have listed, you are tapping into what goes into building confidence. Now let's explore what it takes to build self-confidence.

▶ **Knowledge and Experience.** The more you know about something, the more confident you become in dealing with it. Remember when you first moved into a new role at work? You were excited about what you would be doing. However, you may also have had feelings of uncertainty regarding how successful you would be in dealing with new responsibilities. What's behind those uncomfortable feelings is your not knowing for sure whether you had the necessary skills, whom you were going to be dealing with, what issues remained unknown, and so on. You lacked the familiarity or knowledge and experience that had supported you in your previous position.

▶ **Success.** Building a solid knowledge base without some successes along the way does little to further self-confidence. Whenever we engage in various life experiences, each of us needs a certain amount of success, where we have achieved a desired outcome through our own endeavors. Receiving compliments and accolades after completing an assignment or delivering a presentation can help build confidence. On a grander scale, such acknowledgments of success as getting a promotion, being recognized with an award, or being handed a merit raise further strengthen and build our confidence.

► **Control.** In order to enhance our self-confidence, we need control. This has two dimensions. First, control relates to having a hands-on experience with a particular project, so that when it is successfully completed, we can attribute the success to our personal efforts and contribution. The second aspect of control is knowing the specific steps that lead to the successful completion of a particular project or task. Having this type of control is extremely valuable because as we all know, once you've been successful, it's important to be able to repeat the success. If we are not aware of what we specifically did to make our success possible, it's frightening to know that we have to repeat it.

► **Spiritual or Religious Beliefs.** Finally, for many people, the spiritual and religious component plays an important role in building self-confidence. Even though it's not typically discussed in the workplace, it's necessary to mention this here because it completes the picture of what it takes to develop self-confidence.

Discussing each of these aspects is important because any one aspect, or a combination of them, will answer the question, "How do I become confident?" It also affects the way we perceive and respond to criticism.

When you are criticized for something but can draw upon successful experiences to the contrary, it's easier to deal with the present criticism and not let it rattle you. The opposite is also true. When you lack a frame of reference to put a criticism in perspective, that criticism can have a bigger punch and hurt you more deeply. We typically find ourselves more vulnerable.

To illustrate, let's return to Yana. If she stood back for a moment and looked at her situation objectively, she would realize that in the past few years, she had successfully used the survey-taking equipment. She had overcome her lack of technical knowledge by relying on expert technicians to accompany her at events. In addition to reflecting on her past successes, she should be clear about what she had done and had needed to do to successfully carry out this assignment. If Yana had sorted out the situation this way, her confidence wouldn't be totally shaken. Because she's a high achiever, it's not unusual that it gnawed at her that she had possibly overlooked something that could have been in her control.

Thus, to avoid emotionalizing criticism, first be sure that the criticism you get is valid and accurate and really not intended as a personal attack. Once you establish that it is valid, consider your level of self-confidence in the particular situation. Recognize that if it's low, you should give yourself a little permission to have made a mistake. At the same time, exercise control by making sure you have accurately assessed the situation by putting the criticism in proper perspective. Ask: "Is this my first time?" Or reflect on whether you've had past successes. In an effort to further arm yourself with confidence, determine if you know what really caused the error or mishap. Most importantly, make sure you have a clear idea of what specific action you need to take to correct the situation and that the action that's required is within your control.

DE-EMOTIONALIZING CRITICISM: MAINTAINING A BIG-PICTURE FOCUS

This second factor is powerful because it enables you to de-emotionalize the criticism by putting the situation in proper context. Of great benefit is learning to use the *2M Simultaneous Focus Quick Charge.* Here you are working mentally with two dimensions, the micro and the macro—hence the name 2M. More specifically, the first *M* refers to the macro, or big-picture, long-term view. The second *M* refers to the micro, or more immediate, short-term perspective. Having a big-picture or a macro focus is essential, but it is not enough; nor is it effective to limit your view strictly to the micro.

Therefore, what's needed to help you de-emotionalize the criticism is to meld the macro and the micro by bringing both into view simultaneously. Think of the 2M Simultaneous Focus Quick Charge as a zoom lens on a camera. As you adjust your imaginary camera lens, you have two choices: You can give equal weight to the entire view, or you can emphasize the perspective that's advantageous in a particular situation or at a particular time—that is, the perspective that allows you to leverage your energies most productively to ensure that a valuable difference is realized.

Next time you are criticized, immediately deploy the 2M Simultaneous Focus Quick Charge. Remember, no one will be able to detect that you are putting this skill to use. As you react emotionally, quickly recognize that you are in the micro or immediate situation. Being upset with yourself for having made a mistake is a normal first reaction. Refocus your lens to immediately allow the macro view to take shape and become clear. While in the macro, ask yourself, for example, if *anyone* is perfect, including you. No one likes making mistakes. You are a human being and imperfect; therefore, making mistakes can be considered a natural and inevitable aspect of life. The best you can hope for is that the mistakes that do arise will be little ones, with minimal effect. Large mistakes or small, the point here is that in the big-picture or macro perspective, mistakes are a given. So once again, you need to give yourself permission to make a few.

Still in the macro, you want to remind yourself to stay open-minded because criticism, while uncomfortable, needs to be examined. The fact remains that learning from your mistakes will make a second mistake less likely. As one executive explained, "You want to get in the habit of absorbing the mistake and remembering the lesson." When you make a point of learning from your mistakes, you are turning criticism into a valuable tool for enhancing your performance and for building strong, trusting relationships. Still remaining in the big picture, it's invaluable to hold on to the perspective that the person cared enough to say something! Even if the criticism is awkwardly delivered or abrupt, it's important to keep in perspective that the easiest thing for the giver is to say nothing at all. Laurie, an HR executive who works for a major Boston-based Fortune 500 company, keeps criticism in perspective by viewing it in most cases as a gift. Her mother drilled into her head all through her youth that whenever you receive a gift, you always say "thank you." Operating with this perspective, Laurie admits, helps her to enter a criticism exchange with a more positive and receptive outlook. If she doesn't like the gift, she can always chuck it!

Now you can readjust your lens with lightning speed to the micro and deal with the situation at hand, knowing that at least for the moment, you are directing your energies most productively to make sure you gain a clear understanding of the criticism and the corrective action needed, along with the value to be gained.

DE-EMOTIONALIZING CRITICISM: INSPECTING WHAT OTHERS SAY

The third factor is making a habit of inspecting what others say. We tend to do this naturally when first entering a relationship, but we need to do it beyond that point as well. If you have a new boss at work, your tendency is to hold on to every word uttered just to make sure you are doing okay. Making sure you are listening is important when you are on the receiving end of criticism. From there, though, you need to go further and inspect what's being said. Consider this for a moment: If you accept praise from someone without inspecting it, then when someone criticizes you, out of habit, you won't inspect the criticism very closely. Instead, you will let it pierce through, and you will personalize it.

To develop the habit of inspecting what others say, use the *Filter Quick Charge*. You do this by first viewing criticism as information or data points—nothing more. That's the very best way to initially look at criticism. After all, you are receiving information, and you are the one who is now in charge of assessing the veracity of what's being said. So after neutralizing the information, inspect what's being said by having the information go through an imaginary filtering device. This imaginary filtering device could be something you're wearing, like a piece of jewelry or an article of clothing such as a belt, blouse, shirt, or jacket. The item that you are wearing becomes your mental filtering device, and it comes with a built-in rechargeable battery, so it runs at all times. Its function is to screen the information you receive from others. Use it to distinguish whether you are receiving facts or opinions. Operate with positive intent as you sort out whether what's being said offers potential value. Make a point to listen for the purpose of understanding in order to grasp what the giver is really trying to tell you.

Listening objectively is important because many of your colleagues, team members, and even bosses are moving at high speed and, thus, at the moment of giving criticism, they may not be eloquent communicators. It's possible some of them routinely fail to think about what message they want to convey. Technology tends to encourage this. Because of tweeting, instant messaging, and the onslaught of emails, people are used to reacting. Use your filtering device to analyze carefully what others are saying, even if the message is positive. For instance, let's say a client to whom you have just given a presentation tells you, "You did a marvelous job." Before accepting that praise, mentally assess for yourself whether or not your evaluation of your presentation agrees with the customer's remarks. If you say to yourself that you agree, then you accept the praise. If your quick mental assessment doesn't agree, you may accept only part of the praise or may reject it altogether. Regardless of your filtering system's conclusion, you politely thank your client for taking the time to comment favorably on your presentation.

The same process operates when the comment is rooted in negativity. Before you accept and act on what the giver is saying, your filtering system activates by asking questions such as: Who is this person? What is her purpose right now? Where is she coming from? Are there specifics to accompany the negative information? Is there anything I can learn from the information? Asking these questions helps you more productively direct your emotions. It lets you focus more on what can be. This filtering system helps to smooth what could be a bumpy road so that you can take appropriate action.

What if you disagree with the criticism after inspection? A word of advice: If you are still in the conversation, you are the one in control as the receiver. But that can flip, in a manner that can prove regrettable. It isn't always wise to immediately jump into the mode of "let's set the record straight." Remember that there are many rounds, just as in a boxing match. So carefully weigh what is happening at the moment and then decide what action to take moving forward. Avoid focusing on being right and winning a battle at the expense of losing the war. Situations are fluid. You may find yourself in a meeting with a customer and his team, and he misrepresents something minor that you said in front of the group. This may not be the best time to try to get that error corrected. You can always set the record straight later on, behind closed doors.

Keep in mind that there is a learning phase associated with this Filter Quick Charge, as well as with the 2M Simultaneous Focus Quick Charge. It could take a week before you feel comfortable using these quick charges and managing your emotions more effectively. In the case of criticism from workers with which the relationship is already tense, it may take longer. Even if you have reached the point where you've mastered these quick charges, don't be disappointed if you slip up every now and then. Remember, in the macro picture of the 2M Simultaneous Quick Charge, you aren't perfect!

All told, these three defusing factors—keeping self-confidence high, maintaining a big-picture focus, and inspecting what others have to say—and accompanying techniques work nicely together. Consider your level of confidence at the moment of criticism. If it is low, that's all the more reason to inspect what is being said. Next, put what's happening in the context of the bigger picture. Remind yourself that you are not perfect and that the person may have had good intentions when she took the time to say something. You are only receiving information, so you can at any time reject what's said.

Let's return to the scene introduced at the start of this chapter.

Yana, the high-potential manager, has had an equipment failure at an important conference involving all of her boss's peers. If Yana were equipped with these three de-emotionalizing skills and we could go behind the scenes and examine what went through her mind, we would discover that in a flash she would have utilized the Filter Quick Charge to inspect what Liz just said. Yana would have viewed the words "you let me down" as merely information. Zooming out to the macro picture of the 2M Simultaneous Focus Quick Charge, she would have felt bad because for years she has prided herself on fulfilling all her bosses' expectations. While still in the macro picture, she would wade through a flood of thoughts and would ask herself a variety of questions such as: Did I purposely try to disappoint Liz? Have I successfully utilized the poll-taking devices in the past? Does Liz think I am incompetent? What was my last performance review rating? As Yana gathers information, she is objectively able to stabilize her confidence and gain control over her emotions.

Still remaining in the big picture of the 2M Simultaneous Focus Quick Charge, Yana would get past focusing on herself and would start assessing the general situation. This would get her thinking about what she and the technician could do to try to remedy the situation. Instantly, she would return to the micro, or situation at hand, and apologize to Liz. Mentally returning to the macro picture, she would examine the situation and conclude that Liz was upset and that Yana was the only person Liz could show her frustration to without much risk of jeopardizing the relationship. In realizing this, Yana is able to determine that Liz's delivery of criticism was poor. To let go of the emotional debris, Yana would rely on some additional proven quick charges (which are described in Chapter 8).

Even when the event has passed, Yana's mind would replay the incident dozens of times, repeatedly asking herself what she had overlooked or what she could have done differently. Where was the lesson, she wonders, in this disappointing and unanticipated event? Her bad feelings would eventually be transformed into acceptance as she concludes that there was virtually nothing more she or the technician could have done. The only things that could have been done differently, she concludes, were to have a backup set of poll takers or to outsource the AV equipment. Her only final action step was to pass all this by her boss. Perhaps Liz could offer an option she hadn't considered. By and large, Yana would also accept whatever consequence may result because she acknowledges that it was her responsibility and she was accountable for the outcome.

Because criticism implies the need to take action and since Yana is in control, she decides to bring the topic up a couple of days later when she stops by her boss's office:

Yana: Liz, once again I am so sorry about what happened at the meeting. I've assessed and reassessed the situation numerous times. *(She explains all the precautionary steps that were taken.)* The only thing that could have been done differently is having a backup set of poll takers. Or, in the future, we could hire an outside company to handle the equipment. I don't know what else we could have done.

Liz: Yana, we are not going to invest in another unit. This is the first and hopefully the last time we will encounter such a mess. You did your best. By the way, I apologize for what I said. I was just so upset at the time.

Yana: That's okay, Liz. I understand. Well, thank you. *(The topic of the conversation changes.)*

Yana gets credit for recognizing that saying you're sorry when you are the receiver of criticism is not enough. In the words of the nineteenth-century British statesman Benjamin Disraeli, "Apologies only account for that which they do not alter."[4] Yana invested her energies toward determining what could be done about the situation to prevent it from happening in the future.

Learn to hold in your mind these three de-emotionalizing factors and techniques. Similarly, remember that as an adult you are not going to grant someone so much control over you as to cause you to say or do something you will later regret. You are bringing Eleanor Roosevelt's famous quote (noted at the beginning of this chapter) to life because now you understand what she meant when she declared that another person cannot make you feel inferior unless you allow him to.

AVOID GETTING ENTANGLED IN PERCEIVED CRITICISM: A CLOSE RELATIVE OF SELF-CRITICISM

The criticism that Yana received was up front and in her face. But what about criticisms that remain silent and that we conjure up by ourselves? These are what I refer to as "perceived criticisms."

Here are a few scenarios that demonstrate what I'm talking about. You deliver a presentation to customers and afterward, your boss, who is off to another meeting, says, "Good job." Your thoughts? "Why did he say 'good job' and not 'great job'? What didn't he like?" Or someone approaches you and asks for your advice. You gladly go out of your way to be of help, and you hear nothing back. Your thoughts? "She didn't like my advice. She didn't find it helpful and is uncomfortable telling me." Or after interviewing for a position that's a real match with your expertise, you email the HR director and then don't hear anything. Your thoughts? "I felt the interview went well. I wonder if they're not getting back to me because they're considering other candidates." These three examples are all about allowing your imagination to go unchecked, your anxieties to go unanswered—all with the result of perhaps ruining your day. It's amazing how much time and energy these nagging, negative, critical thoughts can consume when but a few simple questions would resolve them all!

As the receiver of this self-imposed criticism, you want to utilize your control by using the Filter Quick Charge. In order to inspect the criticism, first imagine sitting down and recording everything that you are saying. Then inspect the criticism by asking: "Who's delivering the criticism?" You might also ask: "Where is the information coming from?" In an effort to better understand the criticism, ask yourself,

"How old is it?" Also check out if the specifics are valid. After exploring these questions, you should immediately begin to recognize that the criticisms you are conjuring up in your head lack validity. That discovery alone may be all that's needed to let go of these perceived criticisms. However, if you are still having these lingering thoughts and are unsure, you may elect to probe the real potential source of the criticism. Accomplish this by seeking out the giver of the supposed criticism and asking for clarification. Chances are that the giver will be caught by surprise, having not intended to criticize. Typically, she will say, "Oh, I just got so overwhelmed with things. I never had a chance to get back to you," or "I was in a hurry to respond. I had no idea that would cause you to worry." In the end, you clear the air and clear your head. Most importantly, you are utilizing the control that's inherently yours and continuing to keep your emotions in check. It's an easy fix. However, if you operate as though your thoughts are accurate, you can create a script in your mind that mushrooms into a big ordeal and spins out of control.

This is what happened to Scott. While his situation may seem trivial, it happens quite frequently. Here is how it unfolded. Scott sent an email late in the day to a peer, Brian, who worked in another department, asking for some help on a major assignment that was just handed to him. Brian quickly responded using all caps stating that he was currently overwhelmed and couldn't keep up with everything that was on his plate and added, "Did you ever think about giving me a little more lead time on something like this?"

Scott interpreted Brian's email as a dig and shot back a curt response. And that was all it took for a war of emails to ensue. Eventually, Brian's boss was forwarded the entire email trail. At that point, Scott's boss also got sucked into the situation. Luckily, Scott's boss had enough sense to pull everyone together on a teleconference call (the parties were operating out of four different locations) to sort out the issue. As the story unraveled like the woolen threads in a sweater, it was finally discovered that the catalyst that sparked the whole incident was the email Brian had written in all capital letters. When Brian was asked why he used all caps, he said he was tired and didn't want to take time to rewrite the email—so he just sent it! This story demonstrates the importance of being sure to exercise your control by inspecting what's said in an effort to seek out quality information, or you could be creating or imagining a problem where none exists.

AVOID RESPONDING DEFENSIVELY TO CRITICISM

I often find when coaching executives that they are in search of ways to avoid responding defensively or argumentatively to criticism. Perhaps this is an issue for executives because they rarely receive criticism. As such, they may have been allowed to develop poor habits. The same perspective may apply to you, regardless of whether or not you are an executive. You may find that you are rarely on the receiving end of criticism and are thus rusty in how best to respond. As one manager told a recent college graduate who had just entered the workforce, "Just as you need to learn how to bounce back from a failure, you also need to learn how to tactfully handle criticism without responding defensively." Responding defensively is common, but it need not be automatic. Let's take a moment to explore some triggers that may prompt a defensive response.

For starters, there is your basic attitude. If you view criticism as something to always avoid, as opposed to as a communication process that can enable you to grow and develop, you will most likely take a defensive posture.

Likewise, viewing criticism as a confrontation—as in "I have to confront so-and-so about this issue"—can attitudinally position you to take a defensive stance. You draw battle lines such that only one side can win. This comes from a mistaken premise: Criticism and confrontation are not synonymous terms. The purpose of delivering criticism is not to create a situation where there are winners and losers. Instead, with helpful criticism, a giver is delivering information rooted in negativity for the purpose of inspiring you to change your behavior—to do something better, to achieve a desired end result, or else to grow personally or professionally.

Certain words or phrases can spark a defensive reaction. Richard S. Gallagher, in his book *How to Tell Anyone Anything*, points out examples of emotionally charged words or phrases like "I'll be totally honest," "I hate to say this but . . . ," "This is for your own good," "You must . . . ," "You cannot . . . ," or "I'm sorry."[5]

As we discussed previously, how you listen is also a trigger for causing a defensive stance. If you listen in an argumentative or judgmental way, you are automatically creating a right/wrong, agree/disagree condition. Placing a lot of emphasis up front on whether or not you agree with the criticism will surely position you to respond defensively, especially if you disagree with the criticism. Just as important is paying too much attention to who is giving it and how the criticism is being delivered.

Being aware that you respond defensively and knowing what your triggers are is a good first step. From there, you might try breaking the habit by listing on a sheet of paper those individuals in the workplace to whom you have responded defensively in the past. These are the individuals who arouse your emotions more than others. Then prepare a nondefensive approach and memorize it. You know what it's like when you are in a heated situation and you feel yourself growing more and more upset. It's hard to put together a clear message, pick your words carefully, and still stay engaged in the conversation. Having your message memorized takes less effort and enables you to be more effective.

In communicating with someone to whom you have said things you later regretted, you might prepare yourself by saying at the very beginning of the conversation that you prefer to listen and not simply react as you have in the past. Gain agreement or an okay from the other person before moving forward. Don't assume that remaining silent is acceptable. As the giver starts to deliver his message and you find your emotions starting to boil like water in a pan over a high flame, quickly zip your lips to avoid speaking first and regretting it later. Take a sip of water or drop a pencil on the floor to buy yourself some time. Simply pause for a moment.

When you feel yourself calming down, ask yourself what you want to do as an end result. What are you ultimately looking to achieve?

Remember, you are dealing with two matters: the issue at hand and the other person or people involved in the exchange. The control lies with you. Remember also that no one has a gun pointing at your head forcing you to speak. If you find you're going to explode, then excuse yourself and come back with a cup of water. Another alternative is to offer to end the conversation with the understanding that you will pick up the matter at a later time. You'll find that most givers will respect your wishes. Those who don't either view the situation as urgent or possibly have other less honorable intentions—in which case they should be handled even more cautiously.

Learning to manage your emotions and use them as an asset is very much a skill. As you have read about the skills introduced throughout this chapter, you may have realized that some of them are familiar to you. All the better. But knowing them isn't the whole story: It's using them effectively and getting the desired results that counts. So keep in mind as you try to use these skills that you should not be discouraged if you have difficulty the first few times you use them. Simply understand that as with any new skill, you won't get it right the first or even the second time. It takes practice.

LETTING GO OF A NEGATIVE SITUATION

When you don't live up to your own standards or don't achieve something after working hard, you need to harness your emotions and let go of the negative situation, or "absorb the mistake" by putting into practice three easy-to-learn and easily implemented skills. You've already learned the 2M Simultaneous Focus Quick Charge. The other two skills are the *Wastepaper Basket Quick Charge* and the *"So What? What Now?" Quick Charge.*

As you recall, quick charges are skills that you use instantly in situations without detection from others. The 2M Simultaneous Focus Quick Charge is effective at helping you temper your self-criticism and quickly put a mistake in perspective. Imagine that you just realized that you forgot to do something or you snapped back at someone at the office. You might automatically say to yourself, "How could I be so dumb?" Before you go too far down that path, turn instead to this quick charge. Zoom into the macro picture of the 2M and ask yourself, "Five years from now, how important will this situation be?" Answering this question instantly puts the situation in perspective and helps you realize how insignificant the mistake really is. Now you easily regain your focus and are positioned to address the situation at hand (or the micro) and determine the appropriate action to take.

You will find that when you step aside mentally, a situation that at first seems terrible may suddenly become humorous. Once I had friends over for dinner and decided to prepare a new dish—a fancy soufflé. For what seemed like hours, I kept watching the soufflé, hoping it would rise the way it was supposed to. It finally did, and I removed it from the oven and triumphantly presented it to my husband and friends. When my husband tasted it, he wrinkled up his face but said nothing at first. A moment later, he blurted out, "Oh my gosh, this thing tastes like the ocean!" I tasted the soufflé, and my thoughts about becoming a great chef quickly vanished. It was saltier than the rim of a margarita glass. Even my girlfriend chimed in and said that it was inedible. As we agreed about how awful the soufflé tasted, I realized I had misread the recipe and used tablespoons of salt instead of teaspoons! Even though I had figured out what had happened, my mind was flooded with thoughts about how stupid I was and how I had ruined the evening. I was so embarrassed. But once I thought about the situation in the macro picture, I could only laugh. Instead of beating myself up, I saw the humor in the situation. Luckily, no one was going to go hungry—we just called out for pizza! To this day, my friends and husband enjoy teasing me about my inedible soufflé.

To let go of emotional debris, you want to practice the Wastepaper Basket Quick Charge. This skill is extremely effective if you are a visual person and like to picture things in your mind. To start, envision a sheet of poster board (or paper). Take no more than fifteen seconds to mentally scribble on the poster board the negative thoughts you are having at the moment. Why only fifteen seconds? Because most people can do a royal job of beating themselves up in only a few seconds. Fifteen seconds is plenty of time to make all your negative comments about the situation. Let's say you sent a rough-draft email of a report to your boss to review. Within minutes, he has pointed out in a return email several simple mathematical errors you made in the report. These are errors you should have caught. Even though your boss didn't yell or say anything in his email, you start yelling at yourself. At that point, your best friend is the Wastepaper Basket Quick Charge. Take up to fifteen seconds to mentally write down your negative thoughts: "How could I have been so stupid? Why didn't I double-check my figures? I should have caught that. My boss will think I'm an idiot." Whatever is on your mind at that point gets scrawled on the poster board. At the end of the fifteen seconds, envision yourself taking a very big paintbrush and painting a large *X* across those negative thoughts. Then picture a big wastepaper basket. Take the poster board, crumble it up or tear it into pieces, and dump it into the basket. Then light an imaginary match and mentally burn the whole thing. Depending on the severity of the situation, you may need to repeat the dumping and burning of the poster board a couple of times.

If you are more auditory than visual and often talk to yourself, you might find the "So What? What Now?" Quick Charge to be of greater benefit. Practicing this quick charge involves two steps, where you say:

1. "So what if . . . ?"

2. "What now?" or "What am I going to do about it?"

Let's consider a situation where you are a board member volunteering your time at a charitable organization. During the monthly board meeting, you let your emotions get the best of you and interrupt a fellow board member, declaring how worthless his idea is. Instantly, the mood in the room turns icy and everyone falls silent. During that very awkward pause, you quickly reflect on what just happened. To practice the "So What? What Now?" Quick Charge, say to yourself, "So what if I lost my head? So what if I interrupted this board member and said that his idea was stupid? So what if other board members think poorly of me?" Once again, you go through a mental litany of things you feel like saying to yourself for a set period of time. It's recommended that you limit yourself to five seconds with this skill in most cases. Save the bigger time expenditures for the really big mistakes. At the end of the timed period, follow up by asking yourself, "What now?" or "What am I going to do about it?" Raising this question shifts you from acknowledging your feelings and thinking about what has happened to thinking about how best to deal with the situation. In the next step, you realize that since your fellow board members and others at the meeting heard and understood your hasty words, there's no way to erase them. You figure out that at this moment, the only control you have is to apologize. Upon reflection, you may think about how you got to this point in the first place and what signs you could recognize to help you avoid similar outbursts in the future. You may also conclude that what you want to do about the situation is to call each board member in a timely manner and apologize.

How could you use the "So What? What Now?" Quick Charge to help you recover from the mathematical errors you made in that report to your boss? You might say, "So what if I missed those errors myself? So what if I look careless and unprofessional?" Then you follow this up by asking yourself, "What now?" Very simply, you are addressing what you are going to do about it. Here again, you can't erase the mistake. The only control you have is to quickly make the corrections. To manage your image with your boss, you may decide to hand deliver (if possible) the correct report and thank him for pointing out the errors. At the same time, you may try to assure him that you normally catch those kinds of things. If it's relevant, you may want to offer a brief explanation as to how the errors occurred. When you point out how the errors were made, it lets your boss know that you thought about what happened, and when you propose a plan for how to avoid similar mistakes in the future, he will view you with greater respect. After all, everybody makes mistakes.

The "So What? What Now?" Quick Charge and the Wastepaper Basket Quick Charge are both proven tools for letting go of a mistake or disappointment. However, at first glance, you may not be too excited about using these two quick charges. At least that was the case with one executive during a workshop I was conducting. He found both of them to be somewhat basic and almost childish, especially the Wastepaper Basket Quick Charge. He said very clearly and concisely, "I haven't used crayons and paper and paintbrushes since I was in kindergarten." When he paused, I immediately responded to him as I would to you if you raised the same objection: In the big picture (or when you zoom out to the macro in the 2M Simultaneous Focus Quick Charge), the focus is not whether or not you like or want to use these two skills. What's of utmost importance is that you have acquired a set of skills that you can rely on to enable you to effectively let go of mistakes, disappointments, or other negative situations that come your way. That's where to direct your energies.

In the big picture, it's helpful to make a pact with yourself that gives you permission to make mistakes—after all, you are not perfect. From there, be sure to turn the mistakes into learning experiences where you ultimately formulate the appropriate action to remedy the situation. Along with feeling empowered and more self-confident, you will be practicing what I learned years ago from a most memorable interview with Johnny Bench, the two-time National League MVP who is considered by many to be the best all-round catcher in baseball history. He informed me, "It's okay to make a mistake . . . only once!"[6]

Quick Review for Easy Recall

► To take control of your emotions, use quick charges—easily self-adjusting, neatly packaged techniques used instantly in situations to help you direct your energies more productively.

► Recognize that self-confidence is at the root of exercising control in the handling of criticism. If your confidence is low, you can give it a boost.

➤ To de-emotionalize criticism, arm yourself with confidence by making sure you have a clear idea of what caused the error and that you know specifically what you need to do to correct the situation.

➤ De-emotionalize criticism by putting the situation in proper context using the 2M Simultaneous Focus Quick Charge, giving you both a short-term and longer-term big-picture view of the criticism.

➤ De-emotionalize criticism by inspecting what others say using the Filter Quick Charge, seeing criticism as information or data points that must go through an imaginary filtering device.

➤ Beware of becoming entangled in perceived criticisms where your imagination goes wild and the process consumes a lot of your energy.

PART THREE

Using Criticism for Positive Change

CHAPTER 7

Managing Work
and Volunteer Teams

The Crucial Role Criticism Plays

> *Finding good players is easy. Getting them to play as*
> *a team is another story.*[1]
>
> —CASEY STENGEL

Just as coaches in sports need to have a clear picture of what it takes to win, today's business leaders—in both the for-profit and nonprofit environment—need to know how a successful team is built from the commitment of individuals to come together.

As a manager or team leader, what do you consider to be the main ingredients for successful interaction and integration? It is worth pausing here to write down your thoughts on this topic.

As you create and review your list, you probably have included some of the following:

- ► Goals need to be clearly defined and shared by all team members.

- ► Team members have to know they are charged with accomplishing the goals and must show commitment to achieving them.

► All team members have clearly defined roles and responsibilities.

► Each member has the necessary skills and expertise to accomplish her respective role.

► There is support from top management to achieve the goals.

► Team members must listen to one another and display mutual respect.

► Individuals need to encourage their fellow team members to achieve and must make an effort to ensure that all team members are included in team communications.

These statements touch on and capture what we've found to be the essential factors that consistently go into successful team performances.

Now let's look back at experiences you have had with teams, either as a leader or a member. What do you recall about the route to effective performance? Does your recollection include open communication, where team members were comfortable expressing what they truly believed, even if it meant challenging each other's ideas? Have you been in situations where team members could speak candidly without fear of being identified as negative, a troublemaker, or a naysayer? Regardless of whether the topic was working through a problem, developing a strategy, or exploring an idea, were team members listening for the unbiased purpose of understanding how what was said might affect the achievement of the team's goals? Were team members flexible and willing to change their minds? To put a finer point on it, did team members recognize that they needed to enter meetings with the mind-set of being part of the solution, as opposed to coming into the meeting *with* the solution? After robust exchanges, did the team experience an outcome that was better than what was originally proposed? Did individuals who proposed ideas that were shot down emerge without any feelings of resentment or that they somehow lost status with the group? Did team members lose track of who said what because energies were focused on resolving or working through whatever was on the agenda? As our research shows, in addition to the ingredients listed at the beginning of the chapter, these are all also critical behaviors and attitudes that mark successful teams.

THE SUCCESSFUL TEAM: HOW TEAMS HANDLE CRITICISM MAKES THE DIFFERENCE

If we observe long enough, we may see members of teams behave in a variety of ways regarding criticism. For example, when team members are interacting, one person is dominating or trying to dominate. We may see a team member who is passionate about a particular position and is becoming impatient, stubborn, and prone to interrupting. Still other team members may roll their eyes and sigh whenever a particular individual is about to speak. There may be a team member who is frequently interrupted and whose comments are smugly disregarded by the group. On other occasions, we may see a few team members holding up the team because they are late, or there may be incidences where assignments are not delivered on time or the work quality is substandard. What does all this tell us?

Such behaviors simply tell us that criticism, delivered in subtle or obvious ways, is integral to all teams. How teams embrace criticism can make the difference in whether they achieve stated goals—regardless of individual members' skills or how dedicated the team seems to be. An impractical idea or substandard work on the part of one of the members almost always generates criticism. It can be harsh and direct or delivered indirectly, as when a team member squints with disapproval, rolls his eyes, or sighs as an expression of impatience. The fact that teams can't escape criticism, however, isn't bad. It's a *good* thing!

Leaders and members of teams need to recognize the productive role criticism can play.

A message leaders need to convey, whether for volunteer or work teams, is that to be successful, team members do not only need to be accountable for what they do. They also need to be accountable for what they say and how they say it. While it's not uncommon to hear that there is "no 'I' in team," teams are still composed of individuals. Each brings her own expertise and experiences, as well as frailties and imperfections. Because criticism is ever-present, what happens when team leaders and teams are ineffective at handling criticism? Here are three snapshot scenes that may appear very familiar to you.

Team #1

A fund-raising team was formed to help raise money for a worthy nonprofit community organization. Except for the coordinator leading the effort, everyone on the team was a volunteer. To plan and run the team's fund-raising event, it was deemed necessary for volunteers to divide a variety of responsibilities among themselves. All were expected to do their part and meet deadlines. It became apparent that some of the team members were falling behind schedule, yet they were not being held accountable by the coordinator. Because of the delays, other volunteers began falling behind their schedules, and frustration levels began to build. The volunteers were told that action would be taken to remedy the situation, but nothing seemed to change. So volunteers who were passionate about the project and committed to achieving the desired financial outcome started to pick up the slack themselves. A few ended up putting in extra hours on a regular basis. They became resentful because the coordinator never asked the slackers to pick up the pace. Soon, the more committed volunteers stepped in, took the lead, and started directing the other team members. Resentment and resistance further set in when the team members who were now being directed by other volunteers didn't like being bossed around by "self-anointed leaders." Small cliques were created as various volunteers attempted to form common bonds. Trust and respect eroded and fear set in, as many of the volunteers started to worry about the failure of the entire project.

At the core of these seemingly complicated issues is one main failure on the part of the coordinator, who was the original designated leader—and that is the absence of criticism. What the team did not know at the outset was that the coordinator was "conflict averse," avoiding confrontation at all costs. This set the stage for volunteers to be reluctant to criticize for fear of being rejected and singled out as the naysayers of the group. The sad result was the failure of the project itself.

Team #2

Let's shift to the workplace of a highly skilled team engaged in an important development that could dramatically change existing technologies in the telecommunications industry. Time and budgetary considerations are tight. As a result, team members are under intense pressure to deliver. As they begin to work on the project, tensions mount between those on the design and technology sides. During meetings between the two groups, harsh words are not uncommonly exchanged. Conversations and comments become personal. Egos get involved, and battles emerge over which side is right. A kind of culture sets in where whoever loses the battle this week is dedicated to getting even at some point during the following week.

Team members begin to question the motives of individual players as trust levels plummet. A question arises: Are recommended approaches sincerely designed to encourage the project's success, or are the ideas intended to prove someone wrong in an attempt to embarrass another team member and get even? Under this stress, the team loses its focus. Important issues aren't addressed. Deadlines are missed. To address the open warfare, the leader accuses team members of acting childish and reminds everyone that they are professionals and should act that way.

After a few brief lectures by the leader that only touch the surface, team members fail to take any corrective action and instead resort to more subtle ways of dealing with one another. Backbiting and subterfuge become common. At critical checkpoint meetings, some team members are absent—effectively boycotting the meeting. Their argument is: "Who wants to go to a meeting and get harassed or belittled?"

For this team, criticism isn't absent from the communication process. It's alive and well—only it's used to tear at the fabric and diminish productivity, not to assist it. The leader believes that when he directs his criticisms only at technical matters rather than individual behaviors, the project will move forward and problems will eventually be alleviated. In this case, the leader appears to be more concerned with the intricacies of the technology than how the team is functioning. He is unable or unwilling to see how the ineffective and abusive use of criticism within the team has jeopardized the project.

Team #3

The leader of a circuit board design team promotes and maintains a spirit of family among team members, who consistently show that they are willing to help each other out. The "family spirit" that hovers over the team like a bubble has created a situation in which no one wants to confront (i.e., criticize) anyone for fear of hurting feelings and marring the atmosphere. Consequently, if someone performs work at a mediocre level or incorrectly, team members do not say anything to the person. Rather, they cover for the person and either do it themselves or ignore the mediocre work. While respect among team members is evident, trust in one another is at times questionable. If a team member asks a peer for an opinion, her positive response is questioned because the team member isn't sure if she is trying to be nice and "going along to get along" or if her response is genuine. It's not unusual for deadlines to slip. The overall output of the team is only average.

In this setting, the leader and members of the team aren't necessarily opposed to criticism. It's more a matter of failing to consider when and if criticism has a part to play in their family atmosphere. Consequently, mediocrity often creeps into the team's output, and team players continue to be nice to one another as they operate with a false, yet positive, front that everything is fine.

As these three scenarios show, avoiding or mishandling criticism, whether in a volunteer or work team, breeds institutional dishonesty. In place of objective discernment, there is a holding back of ideas and information or the construction of walls between team members and groups. The ineffective use of or absence of helpful criticism erodes trust and respect, negatively affects morale, and—most important to any leader—can eventually jeopardize the success of the project or mission.

THE DIFFERENCES BETWEEN WORKPLACE AND VOLUNTEER TEAMS

Up to this point, we've described volunteer and work teams with no differentiation. Is there a difference between volunteer teams in the nonprofit sector and for-profit teams in the workplace? Let's take a look.

As we've described, nonprofit volunteer teams and profit-driven work teams share many similarities. They both require clearly defined goals that team members are charged with achieving. In both scenarios, responsibilities and roles need to be clearly spelled out. Teamwork is another common requirement. Furthermore, volunteer groups and workplace teams are not exempt from team criticism!

So where are they different? The main difference lies in the potentially preemptive attitudes of the leaders and team members. With workplace teams, leaders and team members presume that their role and the achievement of particular goals are essential to continued employment. For volunteer teams, the pressure to accommodate the achievement of goals may vary from one person to another. Likewise, what motivates volunteers and what's important to them may be more varied and less apparent. If volunteers don't like the way things are going, they can simply walk away. Furthermore, because a paycheck is not at risk, some volunteers may be more willing to express discontent. They can do so with little risk.

The leaders of volunteer teams need to recognize the importance of establishing proper boundaries and expectations in their teams. These leaders are likely to encounter more unspokens regarding commitment of time and dedication to achieving goals. In fact, the more unspokens there are, the more a leader walks on eggshells. If an atmosphere of boundaries and expectations hasn't been well established, it's not unusual for leaders to hold back on criticizing a volunteer who fails to deliver on a commitment. Without creating a proper environment for acceptance of criticism, a leader who attempts to hold volunteers accountable and calls them out for failing to follow through may find his criticisms rejected because the volunteer views them as out of bounds. Volunteers may feel that such a leader has no clear right to criticize them when they are freely offering their time and expertise. The hesitancy to criticize often results in volunteer leaders making excuses for a volunteer, which leads to reassigning the task to another volunteer or more likely to completing the task themselves. This way, the leaders avoid the risk of offending or, even worse, losing that volunteer.

What all this leads to is that leaders of volunteer teams need to pay special attention to the expectations between themselves and their team members, and they need to direct their energies toward creating an atmosphere of acceptance for criticism. What's more, they need to be even more eloquent in their delivery of criticism so that receivers are not offended or embarrassed and instead are inspired to want to take action. Just as individuals in a relationship need to create an atmosphere of acceptance for criticism, so do leaders of teams. Creating an atmosphere of acceptance for criticism in a team setting starts with promoting open communication where it is made clear that criticism is an integral part of that communication process.

OPEN COMMUNICATION IS KEY

For both types of teams, criticism plays an integral role in enhancing team performance and strengthening teams. For criticism to be effective, however, open communication is key. People must feel that what they have to say is listened to. If you promote open communication within your team, criticism will be considered inbounds and will be used to guard against complacency. In the following sections are ideas worth implementing to establish a foundation of open communication.

Clearly Define and Communicate Your Role as a Leader

To promote open communication where criticism helps to foster an environment built on trust, respect, and camaraderie, leaders need to be sure their role is well defined. While it may seem that the role of a leader is obvious, leaders do have a choice in how they execute that role.

Consider what I refer to as the leader-driven role. That's where the leader drives the team and takes on the responsibility of holding team members accountable. If there are disputes between team members, missed deadlines, or conflicts about which direction to move, the team looks to the leader to be the arbitrator and provide the necessary guidance. After all, if leaders are ultimately accountable for the outcome of their team, then they need to oversee the team and how it functions.

The alternative, in a "team-centric" environment, is to take on more of a "team coach" role where the leader looks to the members of the team to hold each other accountable for how they interact with one another and how the overall team functions. As issues and challenges arise, the leader guides team members with the understanding that it's up to them to resolve issues and to take on the challenges by making the final decisions.

Here's a quick example to illustrate the differences in the two leadership approaches, realizing that one role isn't necessarily better than the other. A team member has missed a deadline for the third time. In a leader-driven approach, the leader would address the situation by approaching the team member about the missed deadlines in an effort to resolve the problem. In a team-centric environment where the leader sets himself up as the coach, the leader would bring the issue back to the team and raise the issue by asking why no one on the team has said anything about the missed deadlines and, most importantly, figured out a solution.

What's key for leaders is clearly understanding what role they are trying to fulfill and being sure that the team accepts that role. When leaders consistently uphold the role, confusion is minimized and team members know how best to utilize and work with their leaders.

A frequent question that's raised with teams is when to criticize the team as opposed to criticizing an individual. Once again, addressing this question depends on the leader's role. For a leader who prefers to have the team be the problem solver and decision maker, the question is best addressed by considering the extent to which the issue impacts the team itself. It's up to the leader and the members of the team to make that judgment call.

For the leader-driven approach, a good rule of thumb is that if the issue involves three or more members of the team, then it's acceptable to bring up the issue to the entire team. If only one or two individuals are at fault, then the situation may best be handled on a one-to-one basis.

Create a Team Atmosphere for the Acceptance of Criticism

Because teams are more complex today, it's important for leaders to make sure that the essential success ingredients are present and viable. Take the need to establish common goals. Just because the goals are stated doesn't automatically mean that everyone has bought into them. Leaders must never assume that stated goals are credible and bought into by all team members.

Likewise, as the three team-related scenes presented earlier illustrate, leaders can't assume that team members (even those with a lot of experience) are automatically on the same page with regard to criticism. Creating an atmosphere where criticism serves as a valuable influencing tool to build strong relationships between bosses and their direct reports involves establishing mutually understood and agreed-upon expectations. Creating such an atmosphere for teams requires the same exercise. With teams, it translates into building "team rules of etiquette," "team guidelines," or "team-run rules."

Here are some examples of effective team rules or a kind of team constitution that all team members adhere to as it relates to the effective use of criticism:

► **Avoid public name-calling.** Be sure that team members understand that it's off-limits or out of bounds to publicly call other team members "stupid," "dumb," "ridiculous," etc.

► **Don't throw someone under the bus.** Such behavior is not acceptable. Be sure that team members understand that the team won't tolerate it when team members blame one another in order to look good or save themselves.

► **Openly admit mistakes.** It's best for team members to recognize that admitting a mistake up front, as opposed to waiting until questioned, is the way to go.

► **Assume positive intent.** Assuming positive intent on the part of other team members encourages listening and discourages a defensive response. Make it known to the team that as problems arise and they make efforts to sort out what occurred, an individual's name often crops up and becomes part of the dialogue. When this happens, it's important that the intent of the giver is to move the problem-solving process along as opposed to trying to incriminate the individual and cast blame.

► **Do not shoot the bearer of bad news.** When team members "shoot" the bearer of bad news, not only are they delivering unfair criticism—they are also promoting an atmosphere that discourages openness and honesty. Be sure the team buys into this rule, which in essence says: "Be glad the information is being communicated."

► **Don't engage in hindsight criticism.** If a team decision turns out poorly, it's out of bounds to say, "I told you so." To make decisions, the team needs to work with 60 percent agreement and 100 percent commitment. Once the team makes a decision, everyone is in—no after-the-fact or hindsight criticism.

► **Go to the source.** Explain that it's out of bounds to talk negatively about other people behind their back. If something is bothering team members, explain that they need to go directly to the source.

► **Don't criticize via email.** Using email to criticize someone in the workplace is not an effective way to build relationships. *Pick up the phone!* Criticizing by email is out of bounds because if the message is misinterpreted, a minor situation can escalate and easily become a big one.

► **Give credit where credit is due.** This rule says to voluntarily look for opportunities to praise or reward others. When something is done successfully, those who did the work need to get the credit. In addition, it's out of bounds to take credit for something you did not do.

Schedule "Idea Only" Meetings

A big question that leaders need to ask themselves and their teams is when to take a "time-out to think." Scheduling meetings periodically throughout the year for the purpose of generating ideas is an important investment of time. When setting up these creative sessions, leaders and their team members need to decide if the criticism of ideas is allowed. Just the idea of permitting criticism may initially sound unacceptable, especially if the team is a believer in brainstorming.

Charlan Nemeth, a psychology professor at the University of California, Berkeley, claims that contrary to popular belief, criticizing ideas yields better results than the traditional practice of brainstorming. In research conducted in 2003, Nemeth divided female undergraduates into teams of five, posed the same problem-solving task to each team, and then assigned each set of teams one of three conditions. One set of teams received standard brainstorming instructions, including the condition that no criticism was allowed. The second set of teams was assigned what Nemeth called the "debate" condition, where both the sharing and criticizing of ideas was allowed. The third set of teams was given no instructions whatsoever. Results showed that when groups were allowed to engage in the debate condition— where team members were allowed to discuss and criticize ideas— they produced an average of twenty-five more ideas than the teams that followed the traditional brainstorming techniques.[2]

Well-handled criticism, where people are allowed to fight about ideas, can serve as a catalyst to inspire team members to do better and thereby create ideas that are meaningful and show promise. David Burkus, an author and expert on teams, throws in a caveat. He says, "It's important that you're engaging in the 'right fight,' criticizing another person's ideas and not the person himself."[3] For this type of conflict, there needs to be an atmosphere of mutual respect, and the focus needs to be on the task itself where fact-based data get presented. Having periodic meetings in which criticism is accepted promotes open communication and can help teams avoid becoming stagnant.

Establish a Process Whereby Team Members Assess How Well the Team Is Functioning

If the training and HR departments don't have any instruments to assess how well teams are functioning, leaders can easily develop their own questionnaires and other tools. If the team has truly integrated open communication and in the process created an acceptance for criticism, then the leader can schedule a meeting totally devoted to assessing how well the team is doing, including an assessment of the individuals who make up the team. Sometimes having a facilitator is helpful during an assessment because the leader can be treated as part of the team. Furthermore, the facilitator can keep the team on topic even as challenging questions or issues are raised. A well-briefed facilitator might remind the team of mistakes or wrong directions taken in the past, recalling the adage "How can you know where you are going if you don't know where you've been?" Scheduling these meetings sends a strong message that openness, transparency, and candidness are important.

In addition, when members of the team subscribe to "open communication," then communicating candidly with one another, whether from the leaders or team members' perspective, is an everyday occurrence. These formal assessment meetings serve as a team's time-out to reveal how the team is doing from a "10,000-foot level." It's not about bringing up a topic or issue that has been stored in a desk drawer for months gathering dust.

Show Leadership by Admitting Mistakes

A leader who is willing to admit mistakes greatly influences how others on the team handle and recover from errors and problematic situations. By admitting a mistake, a leader conveys a clear message that it's human to err. When team members (in both volunteer and work settings) see a team leader admit a mistake, it sets a good example for their own behavior and lays the groundwork for an atmosphere of openness within the team. As a result, team members will be more willing to say something if they see a disaster coming. They will speak with courage and take risks. In a fast-paced, fiercely competitive work team setting, acknowledging an error quickly is valuable for ensuring that no time is lost before correcting it.

Encourage Socializing
Outside the Workplace

If the team is working remotely, it obviously isn't possible for members to socialize outside the workplace unless the leader makes a special effort to periodically bring them together. If the team is centrally located, it's extremely valuable to arrange downtime when team members have an opportunity to feel comfortable socializing with one another. Events like this encourage the broadening of personal boundaries even as they enhance trust and respect. Social togetherness gives team members an opportunity to get to know the person behind the role. It also provides an opportunity for team members to make amends—if amends turn out to be necessary. Research from MIT's Human Dynamics Laboratory quantified what many seasoned leaders already suspect. The researchers found that successful teams communicate frequently outside formal meetings. (The research had nothing to do with the content of the message, simply the frequency.)

Even in tough economic times, leaders can create opportunities where team members can casually get together. All of this helps to create a healthy atmosphere where criticism can gain acceptance. Why? Because when trust and respect are ingrained in relationships, criticism is most likely thought of as having a helpful motive behind it.

Ask for Team Commitment,
but Be Careful

It's not enough for a leader to ask for everyone's commitment to the team's goals because how team members express their commitment varies from one player to the next. To avoid misunderstandings and the buildup of tension between team players, which may serve as a breeding ground for dissent, leaders of both volunteer and work teams need to clarify what that commitment looks like in action. What's the unspoken message for you here? Don't be critical if team members express their commitment differently than you do.

The clients I've worked with over the years have found that team players can be placed in several categories. I call these Committed Crusaders, Silent Knights, Doubting Thomases, and the dangerous Quiet Saboteurs.

Committed Crusaders are visibly excited and typically are the ones who raise their hand when extra help is needed. This is in contrast to the Silent Knights, who are individual team players who are quiet and reserved but just as committed to the project as their demonstrative peers. When asked a question, they have a response, and if asked to volunteer for something, they are always willing. (A word of advice: Leaders who approach Silent Knights and ask them to be more like Committed Crusaders are often met with resistance. These individuals like being Silent Knights.)

And then there are the Doubting Thomases and Quiet Saboteurs. The Doubting Thomases are the ones who put the brakes on just when the leader thinks the team is ready to move. Their questions and concerns typically drive the rest of the team and the leader crazy, but, as so often happens, Doubting Thomases can catch something important that has been left out of the group's thinking and, in the end, members become glad to have had Doubting Thomases on the team. The Quiet Saboteurs, on the other hand, are the team players who say "yes" in the meeting, but outside the meeting they ridicule and criticize what's been said or decided. These are the individuals who are looking to throw a wrench into the project or introduce a surprise that either derails the whole team or negatively targets certain individuals. You get the picture. Leaders who have Quiet Saboteurs on the team should work hard to remove them or put them in a position where they can do little to no damage. They should also watch out for the Doubting Thomas types, because if the leader or other team members either roll their eyes and sigh every time the doubters speak or make them the brunt of jokes, these individuals can become Quiet Saboteurs.

Be Skeptical of Trying to Create a Proper Praise-to-Criticism Ratio

When promoting open communication, the process includes both praise and criticism—but in what proportion? There has been a lot of chatter about the proportion of criticism to praise in teams. Much of this discussion is coming from research that the leadership authorities Jack Zenger and Joseph Folkman published on the ideal praise-to-criticism ratio. They noted the findings of research conducted by academic Emily Heaphy and consultant Marcial Losada, which examined the effectiveness of sixty strategic business unit leadership teams at a large information-processing company. They revealed that the highest performing teams had a 6-to-1 ratio of praise to criticism.[4] While criticism is necessary to all high-performing teams, the team's productivity can erode if criticism seeps into the communication exchange too frequently. The findings show that low-performing teams had three negative comments to every positive one. Before buying into these ratios, it is valuable for leaders to consider that most team members are not skilled in giving or receiving criticism. Because criticism is so powerful, one poorly delivered critique can cause severe damage. So what we do not know from the study is whether the participants were skilled at handling criticism both from a giver's and a receiver's perspective. It would be interesting to study the proportion of well-deserved praise to helpful team criticism, because well-delivered criticism is extremely motivating, especially when it links to team goals and what is important to the team.

Building successful teams is no easy task. Just think about the number of teams that have consistently been successful, whether in sports or in business, and you quickly have an appreciation for how difficult it is. No one has a patent on what goes into a successful team, but it is clearly evident that you cannot have a successful team without the effective use of helpful criticism.

Quick Review for Easy Recall

► Recognize that criticism in subtle or obvious ways is integral to all teams, and that teams who embrace criticism can make the decisive difference in whether they will or will not be successful.

► Consider the fact that team leaders have a choice in how they approach leading the team. They can take the lead as in taking on a "leader-driven" role, or they can function more in a "team coach" role, encouraging team members to be accountable to one another. Whatever the choice, a team leader's role needs to be clear, understood, and accepted by the team.

► Create a team atmosphere for the acceptance of criticism.

   ▶ To ensure that team members are committed to the stated goals of the team, it's best to ask.

   ▶ Establish team-run rules or guidelines to promote a team atmosphere for the acceptance of criticism. Team guidelines can include the following:
   - Avoid public name-calling.
   - Don't throw someone under the bus
   - Openly admit mistakes.
   - Assume positive intent.
   - Do not shoot the bearer of bad news.
   - Go to the source.
   - Give credit where credit is due.

► Schedule "idea only" meetings where criticism of ideas is an acceptable practice.

► Establish a process whereby team members assess how well the team is functioning.

► Avoid misunderstandings and the buildup of tension between team players, which may in turn create a breeding ground for criticism, by explaining what team commitment looks like in action.

► Team members should not be critical of other team members if they express their commitment differently.

CHAPTER 8

Handling Difficult Situations

> *You have to know how to accept rejection and reject acceptance.*[1]
>
> —RAY BRADBURY

Previous chapters of this book have presented a structured thinking process—one that positions you basically to address any kind of criticism. In this chapter, we explore some of the more challenging situations you may encounter as either a receiver or a giver of criticism. Even for people with a decent mastery of the criticism process, it's quite possible to become rattled by unusual situations that go beyond the scope of prior experience. This chapter addresses scenarios that are particularly difficult or awkward. All of them have actually occurred among employees, peers, and leaders in the real-life workplace. You can't make this stuff up!

The situations discussed in this chapter are difficult encounters that may stop you cold when you find yourself either giving or receiving criticism. Many involve a human factor that requires large amounts of empathy, sympathy, and understanding.

You never want to abandon your adherence to the sequential paths shown in the Giver Communication Chart and Receiver Control Chart presented in Chapters 4 and 5, respectively. These charts are always operable and will never let you down, even when urgency and panic are about to set in. Think first, visualize both the Giver Communication Chart and the Receiver Control Chart, then choose your words or deeds.

As a giver, when you are faced with a particularly tough situation or are concerned that the exchange may evolve into an even tougher situation, focus on the receiver side of the issue before beginning an exchange. Your receiver's first thoughts after you deliver the criticism typically are: "Who is this person? Will I accept criticism from him? Do I understand what is being said?" If so, the next thought is: "Is it inbounds?" The questions you as the giver need to address are all covered in the Giver Communication Chart. The sequence may need to be altered when you are mentally rehearsing your delivery (Step III). For instance, the receiver's question about whether the criticism is inbounds, which is one of the first points the receiver will ponder, is the sixth question on the Giver Communication Chart.

These tough situations may take some time to think through. But moving through the Giver Communication Chart will keep you focused. Meanwhile, when you are the receiver, always remember when being criticized that you are in control of the timing and content of your reaction.

Let's delve into what could be some of the more challenging situations you may encounter as both a giver and receiver of criticism.

CHALLENGING SITUATION #1:
The Receiver Doesn't Understand the Criticism

A supervisor manages the housekeeping staff in a large hotel. Most of her workers speak English proficiently, but a significant number are foreign-born and have recently immigrated to the United States. One housekeeper, who is an immigrant from Poland, has been repeatedly walking into guest rooms without knocking first. This has upset the guests, some of whom have called the front desk to complain. The supervisor discusses the problem with the housekeeper, in a manner the supervisor considers complete and specific. Then, when the supervisor hears of further complaints, she feels that the housekeeper has ignored her instructions about knocking before entering. Based on that assumption, the supervisor finds it difficult to address the complaints in a restrained tone, and she comes down on the housekeeper loudly and somewhat angrily. The housekeeper in turn becomes upset, thinking she could lose her job if the circumstance happens again. While the supervisor may have thought she did all she could to make it clear what the housekeeper should do, she learns later from another staff member that the housekeeper never actually understood her instructions. The housekeeper's knowledge of the English language was weak, and she disguised that weakness, fearing it would affect her employment.

Speaking with people who are not fully fluent in the language that's being used goes to the problem of many givers who assume the vocabulary they employ when giving criticism is understood. This might also be true about individuals who have hearing difficulties or have vocabulary issues related to a lower-than-average level of education. Bear in mind that receivers of criticism sometimes act as if they understand what is being said when in fact they don't. As the Giver Communication Chart suggests, you are best off probing the receiver to determine if the message got through. You can ask the receiver to repeat back the corrective action she is expected to take. If you feel that someone has real difficulty understanding you, you might want to use a translator website or another source to help in translating the conversation.

CHALLENGING SITUATION #2:
The Receiver Starts to Cry

You are discussing the unpleasant situation of a key deadline being missed by one of your direct reports. The two of you are alone in your office with the door closed, and you are trying to understand what happened. Feeling overwhelmed, the employee starts to cry. What do you do? Tears and sobbing can be uncontrollable, and their effect is to make both the giver and the receiver of criticism uncomfortable.

Be careful of two things as you envision this situation. First, try not to picture the employee as a woman—men cry, too. Also, try not to assume that the employee is crying because of hurt feelings or in recognition of poor performance. Receivers also cry because of frustration or as a result of tremendous anger welling up inside them. Thus, you should never assume the conditions that exist when someone starts to cry during a criticism exchange.

In actuality, this scene involved a male employee. Too much was happening in his world. He was so frustrated that when his boss brought up the missed deadline, it was the final straw and he couldn't hold back the tears.

When someone you criticize begins to cry, you may think of sending him out of your office to the restroom so he can gather his composure. This is not a good idea. Once the employee steps out in the open workplace, in all likelihood he will come in contact with other employees. That may cause him even more embarrassment. Furthermore, it instantly fuels the rumor mill. Other employees are going to wonder what took place in your office that caused the employee to cry and whether it's something they should be concerned about.

What about handing the employee a tissue? This may seem to be appropriate, but it's not always a good idea. It can easily send the unspoken message of "clean up your act in front of me."

In the midst of an emotional breakdown where crying is involved, it's best for you to simply exit the situation. Explaining that you need to check on something is a tactful way to exit the scene. It's also helpful to let the receiver know when you'll be back (say, in a few minutes). Providing a time estimate reassures the receiver that you will return. It gives him an opportunity to regain his composure and assess what has occurred. By stepping out, you can also assess whether the situation you were originally discussing is urgent. It may be that this is not the best time for the two of you to continue the discussion.

Additionally, if you feel the employee is angry and may lose control, you may want to delay the matter under discussion to another time, provided it can wait. As you may have experienced, it's difficult to engage in a meaningful discussion with a receiver who is not receptive for whatever reason. If it can wait, you may offer the receiver the option to continue or not. However, if the matter is urgent, explain to the receiver the reason why you need to continue the conversation. In each case, your actions will communicate that you are attempting to show compassion for the receiver, all the while keeping in mind the situation at hand. What if the receiver begins to appear angry or aggressive when you resume the conversation? Then, unquestionably, you should ask him to remain in your office so he can compose himself. Meanwhile, you would be wise to seek out a third party, possibly from human resources, to accompany you during the rest of the conversation.

What about the notion of continuing without interruption because you are not bothered by someone's crying? This is what one manager claimed. However, after thinking carefully about what she had said, she realized her comfort level shouldn't be the main focus. At the time, she was dealing with a young female employee who cried every time she was on the receiving end of criticism. The employee had ambitious career aspirations. The manager realized that, in general, crying was not an acceptable workplace response. She told the employee that if she truly wished to advance in her career, the tendency toward crying needed to be addressed.

It's not unnatural for people to cry when they are criticized, regardless of sex, age, ethnicity, or level in the organization. Circumstances in life can well up, and when strain intersects with a sense of being overwhelmed, anyone can cry or feel like crying—even you!

COACHING TIP #15:

Regaining Your Composure
While Encountering Criticism

To help you when tears are welling up in your eyes, whether being criticized or not, try implementing the *Look Up Quick Charge*. This quick charge is practiced by shifting your eyes to look up toward the right. Doing this helps stop the tears. Hold that position for a moment and think of something that's pleasant while continuing to look to the upper right.

Another option to help you regain control is to ask the giver if you could have a moment or two to compose yourself. This way, even if the giver doesn't offer you time to pull yourself together, you can accept control and ask for it on your own behalf. What's valuable in this awkward situation is knowing that you have some control.

CHALLENGING SITUATION #3:
Handling the Explosive Employee

There will be times when it becomes necessary to criticize people you have reason to believe can get quickly upset with most any criticism that comes their way. In these cases, it's valuable to refer to Step II of the Giver Communication Chart and consider if the receiver is capable of any behavioral change.

One top-performing project leader in a well-known defense company resented others on the team who did not deliver quality work on time. Typically, she would approach them when she was upset and bluntly let them know how disappointed she was. Everyone on the team accepted her direct approach because she was extremely competent and cared passionately about the project's success. Even her boss relied on her a great deal because in the end she always delivered the end product. Like the others on the team, he would overlook her emotionally charged manner of criticizing others.

One day, she basically lost all control and exploded at a team member who had failed to deliver an extremely time-sensitive report. When the boss got wind of what happened, he told her flat out that there was no excuse for losing control to that degree. If she did it again, he told her, she would lose her job. At the same time, he believed she was capable of keeping her emotions in check.

So he offered her an opportunity to receive coaching, which she reluctantly accepted. After that, he was pleasantly surprised to see over the next few months that she never had another blowup. When asked what had changed her behavior, she told him that the threat of losing her job opened her up to accepting coaching. She added, "That coach was great! She made me realize that my emotions were getting in my way of career advancement, and she made me see that I was capable of changing how I react to people who don't follow through or do good work. It all made sense to me. While it's my responsibility to hold people accountable, I can do it without operating as a sergeant in the military where I am barking out orders. It's not just about the work, the coach pointed out—it's a matter of my effectively influencing others and treating them with respect."

As this example suggests, understanding the consequences of not changing is a powerful motivator as long as the consequences that are threatened touch on one's goals and aspirations. Likewise, having the organization invest in the employee sends a strong message of support and provides the employee with an opportunity to acquire the skills necessary to improve.

Not all situations are that simple. A staff member considered to be among the company's top technicians was transferred to the team of one manager. Along with his reputation for technical wizardry, the staff member was also known as a big problem because of emotional outbursts. At meetings, he would get so upset and disruptive that sudden adjournment was the only apparent solution. In fact, his former boss couldn't handle him. HR hoped that moving him to another team would give him a fresh start and would alter his behavior. His new manager set up a meeting with the wizard to discuss how best to work around his emotional outbursts. Rather than shy away from the issue, the boss addressed it up front, explaining that on his team, blowing up and causing disruptions was not acceptable behavior. At first, the technical wizard was taken aback. No one had ever approached him this directly. He fought back, saying that he had his own ideas and didn't want to become sheepish and passive like his peers (which was the way he perceived them). The manager was quick on his feet and said, "I'm not trying to change you. I'm trying to change the way we work together, and blowing up is not going to work on this team."

After an involved discussion where they talked about various ways he could handle his emotions, the employee finally agreed that when his emotions started to run high, he would excuse himself to get a drink of water to calm down. For an entire year after making the agreement, the employee excused himself from meetings only twice. And on each occasion, mutual respect and cooperation was maintained between the manager and the technical wizard.

How you handle such situations is up to you when you encounter someone who has a reputation for blowing up or who has an occasional flare-up. Once again, the Giver Communication Chart is your best reference as you think about how to address the situation. In the case of the technical wizard's reputation for being emotionally volatile, the manager's up-front comments were what we call a "clarification of expectations." Another option is waiting until an incident has occurred because you want to give the employee the benefit of the doubt. However, once an incident has occurred, you are delivering criticism after the fact. It's your decision. There's nothing wrong with electing to wait. However, if a blowup does occur, then, when referring to Step II of the Giver Communication Chart, you need to explain to the receiver now what made the criticism inbounds. When you rehearse your delivery as Step III advises, you want to point out that you know about the receiver's reputation, and—very importantly—you need to explain why you delayed the criticism. The reason you want to deliver your message this way is because the receiver's intelligence needs to be respected. The tech wizard knew that his new manager was aware of his reputation. Taking an unspoken (the wizard's tendency to blow up and cause disruptions) and making it spoken put both the manager and the employee on a level playing field from the outset. Using a matter-of-fact tone, which you practiced in Step III of the Giver Communication Chart, sends another message that it's an issue that needs to be handled, as opposed to a formal directive, which rings alarms of potential threat for things that haven't happened yet. And remember, it always helps to smile while laying out expectations.

If you, like the technical wizard, tend to get emotional and occasionally blow up, then having clear parameters set for you, or by you, may be all that is necessary to remedy the situation. However, if that's not enough, there are other things you can do to better manage your emotions. For instance, learn to recognize certain clues, such as interrupting others, talking faster, changing your tone of voice, or feeling as if a balloon is blowing up inside your chest as your breathing becomes more rapid and shallow. These are clues that should alert you that your emotions are getting stirred up. When any one of these signals is present, slow down, stop talking, and pause. If you believe you can regain control of your emotions and remain in the meeting, it may help to consider the end result you are trying to achieve rather than the issue that is causing your stress. On the other hand, if you have difficulty calming your emotions, excuse yourself to go use the restroom or get something to drink.

COACHING TIP #16:

A Secret Way to Maintain Your Cool

To keep your emotions in check when you feel yourself beginning to get anxious and upset while in front of others, make an attempt to put into practice the *Breathing Quick Charge*.

To use the Breathing Quick Charge, inhale deeply through your nose and hold your breath for a second or two, then exhale very slowly through your nose. Combine your exhalation with a relaxation of your whole body, starting at the top of your head when you first start to exhale, and working your way down to your toes. Repeat the process two or three times to instill a smooth rhythm of breathing. Also, when you start to speak, talk more slowly and in a matter-of-fact tone of voice. If you can't do that, then it's a sign that you are about to lose it and may need to zip your lips before you blow it.

By the way, the Breathing Quick Charge can be used alone or with other techniques as part of a strategy to help you direct your energies positively. For instance, you might want to combine the Breathing Quick Charge with the 2M Simultaneous Focus Quick Charge to help you zoom out to the macro picture to quickly regain your focus and objective.

Here's how Marilyn dealt with a tense situation. She entered into a sensitive interdepartmental meeting dealing with customer deadlines that had been missed by a peer of hers from another department who was at the meeting. Soon after the meeting began, the atmosphere got very tense, and colleagues who were familiar with Marilyn and her reputation for having a short emotional fuse got worried and anticipated she would quickly demonstrate her pent-up anger. But to everyone's surprise, when Marilyn's peer started to become loud and defensive, Marilyn stopped talking, paused a moment to reflect on the purpose of the meeting, then said to her peer, "You're getting very excited and that's making me very excited. Can we take a moment to hit the reset button?" The peer quickly became aware of how upset she had become, and both women agreed to stop and revisit the issue at hand. After that, they carried on in a more productive manner.

Whether it is dealing with your own emotions or dealing with the emotions of others, keep in mind that you need to be open to the possibility that the underlying cause of emotional outbursts may not be related to the immediate issue. People who have problems at home, issues with alcohol and drugs, certain medical conditions (such as blood sugar complications), or mental challenges (ranging from depression to various forms of psychosis) can exhibit flare-ups of emotions. Frequent outbursts from people who persistently resist attempts to modify their behavior may require professional help beyond your abilities. That is the reason why it is important to consider Step III where you determine if you are qualified to deliver the criticism.

CHALLENGING SITUATION #4:
You Are Getting Criticized for Doing
What You Were Told to Do

This issue occurs more often than you might think. Given people's long to-do lists and heightened performance demands, it's quite possible that a boss, a peer, or a team member actually forgot something he told you to do and proceeded to criticize you for doing it.

Because of this, you might be wise to give the person the benefit of the doubt the first time he criticizes you for doing something that the giver asked you to do. That's what Terry, a recent hire in a Wall Street investment firm, did. His new boss, Mick, directed him to format the creation of some financial forecasting spreadsheets. Then Mick viciously criticized Terry for doing it—the very thing Mick had asked Terry to do! Nevertheless, the benefit of the doubt soon evaporated when Terry came to recognize that this was a pattern. His boss would think nothing of criticizing Terry for something that he had actually asked Terry to do. At first, Terry was perplexed. Then he began to look at things more closely. He asked himself if the criticism was really about what he was doing and how he was doing it or whether Mick was forgetting what he was telling Terry to do. It finally became apparent to Terry that the matter had nothing to do with mistakes or his failure to follow instructions. He realized that it all had more to do with Mick than with himself. When stepping back and viewing the big picture, Terry realized that this was really just how Mick figured out what he really wanted. Mick could not clearly determine what he really wanted until he had actually seen what Terry had done.

If you are experiencing a situation similar to that of Terry, or if you have experienced this in the past, then you might want to consider some of the following helpful hints to avoid inviting criticism. They have been extremely effective for Terry. To formulate his plan, Terry referred to the Receiver Control Chart, where he paid particular attention to Step II.

For starters, Terry found it helpful to simply summarize in an email to Mick what he was asked to do to make sure he was on the same page with his boss. When possible and appropriate, he included in the email what the final end result would look like. Then he would stop by and visit briefly with Mick to make sure this was what his boss wanted. Sometimes "what" people say they want doesn't always equate with what they are looking for as an end result. So Terry's clarifying particulars and details by pointing them out in writing and reiterating them verbally helped his boss to clarify his thinking. Another valuable tip that Terry used on bigger projects was to break the larger task into smaller parts. As each smaller part was finished, Terry would pass it by his boss for his approval.

To help with feelings of frustration, you, like Terry, may need to be reminded that your job isn't to judge or to change your boss—or your peers, for that matter. Your job is to work with these people. As a result, you need to accept that there may be times when you need to go through two or three reiterations before your boss, peer, or even your customer (let's not exclude them) is satisfied. So plan extra time and don't take what's happening personally as a reflection of your adequacy or competency.

As Terry came to recognize, when dealing with other people, like his boss, you can more accurately assess ways of dealing with different situations by viewing people as they behave, not as they should behave. Couple that insight with verifying that the person's actions really aren't against you but are really more a matter of his management or work style. How can you tell? To address this question, let's use Terry's boss as an example. If this is Mick's management style, then he would be doing the same things with others, not just with Terry. Casual hallway conversations with current and former peers would sort that perspective out. Knowing that it's not about you can lower your emotional fuse and encourage you to develop a viable course of action. Using these insightful premises can help you to think more creatively and use your energies wisely. Plus, making an effort to keep track of what's working and not working helps you to figure out what it's going to take to more effectively interact with people, especially those who are more challenging.

CHALLENGING SITUATION #5:
Dealing with Personal Matters That Are Sensitive, Potential "Inbounds" Issues

As a manager, how do you handle the following workplace scenes?

► The people in your department who deal directly with the public are upset and in a buzz one morning because one of their team members came to work dressed inappropriately. She is wearing flip-flops and a see-through blouse, when the standard unspoken apparel is a business outfit and closed shoes.

► An employee who has terrible breath is the brunt of jokes, even in your presence.

► You hear complaints from other team members about a peer who never says "good morning" to any of them or to customers she is not directly dealing with.

► Your boss stops by your office telling you to say something to one of your reports because he is wearing an oversize earring.

In these cases, you would be dealing with potential inbounds or out-of-bounds criticism issues.

The first thing you need to consider and decide when referring to Step II of the Giver Communication Chart is if the issue is inbounds. There are three criteria by which to judge whether a situation is inbounds. The first is if a policy exists in the company. If so, then it's a definite inbounds issue. Second, there's the question of whether the criticism situation has a negative effect on creating or maintaining a conducive work atmosphere, where employees feel they can be productive and where clients or customers respect the discipline of your workplace. Third, does the situation negatively affect the image that the organization is interested in maintaining?

Let's say a dress code policy exists. Then, in the case of the employee wearing the large earring or the one with the see-through blouse, the criticism is inbounds and needs to be addressed. Before reacting, stop and refer to the Giver Communication Chart to ask yourself if the situation is urgent. In some situations and with some bosses, this answer may be arguable. So, you need to stop and think before automatically reacting. Whether you address the situation immediately or hold off, you need to keep the boss who is urging action on your part informed.

What if no policy exists? Then you need to consider why the situation is inbounds and if it even needs to be addressed. Let's return to the employee who is wearing the oversize earring. When carefully considering the matter, you know that the employee works by himself and has no contact with customers. As you assess the situation further, you realize that the earring doesn't present a safety risk. So in the end, you may decide that the situation doesn't need to be addressed because it's a strictly personal matter. Is it inbounds because the boss asked you to say something? If you are unsure, the Giver Communication Chart suggests that you probe further, which in this case means that it's best to go back to your boss to gain a better understanding of what he had in mind when he approached you about this. After discussing the matter with him, not only will you have a clear idea of what to do but you'll both be on the same page.

If no dress code policy exists, then the situation of the woman with the see-through blouse is likely inbounds because she is part of a team working with the public. You may reach a similar conclusion with the employee who has bad breath, which is another situation that needs to be addressed because it's affecting the work environment and customer relations. But what about the employee who doesn't say "good morning" or offer other pleasantries? If it's not clear to you and you are unsure, then, as the Giver Communication Chart recommends, you need to probe further. This may mean reaching out to your boss, another colleague, or someone in HR to help you work through the matter.

Regarding the employee who doesn't share pleasantries with her colleagues, would you consider the situation inbounds if you were in the hospitality industry? Many who have grown up in the industry subscribe to the "ten-foot rule," which was actually started by Sam

Walton of Walmart. It's the idea that whenever anyone, especially a guest, comes within ten feet of you and makes eye contact, then you need to acknowledge him and ask if there is anything you can do to be of help.[2] Now, is the criticism inbounds? Once again, if it's unclear, be sure to delay saying anything until you speak with your boss or HR representative. After all, it's not urgent!

Up until now, nothing has been said about developing an approach for dealing with these situations. Addressing these situations involves referring once again to the Giver Communication Chart and this time paying special attention to the urgency of the situation, as well as to the question of whether you are the best person to deliver the criticism. Even if you have concluded that a situation is inbounds because it falls within your responsibility to do something about it and it's urgent, you may still not be the best person to deliver the message. Take, for example, the employee who has bad breath. You may conclude that perhaps the employee's bad breath is the result of taking prescription drugs, and in that case, you are not the best person to deliver the criticism. Instead, you may want to ask the employee to go to medical because the issue can be resolved there. If your organization lacks a medical department, then seek out guidance from your boss or HR. Likewise, with the employee who doesn't greet coworkers, you may suggest that those who brought the situation to your attention address it themselves. You may offer to coach them to help ensure they are prepared and can have a productive meeting.

Inbounds and out-of-bounds issues can be tricky, and it is essential to take the time to think about whether or not the receiver will accept the criticism. Just as important is your delivery. It's valuable to mention up front the reason the criticism is inbounds. Take, for example, the sensitive issue of a married employee who is having an affair with someone else in the company and is using no discretion. Everyone is talking about the situation, and it's causing a lot of disruption in your department. You may need to set the stage by clarifying from the beginning with the employee that what he is doing in his personal time is his own business, but when it's public and disrupting overall productivity, then it becomes the company's business. All the while, your purpose is to make the employee aware that his indiscreet behavior is not acceptable.

These are important issues where it may be advisable to consider consulting HR. In each case, examining the urgency of the situation, whether or not it's best for you to address the issue, and factoring in what is necessary for the receiver to be receptive to the criticism are all vital considerations that need to be carefully thought through before anything is said.

CHALLENGING SITUATION #6:
You Want to Avoid Hurting Someone's Feelings

As a giver, whether you're dealing with your boss, peer, team member, or employee, even if your intent is to be helpful, it's not unusual to feel some angst over the possibility of hurting someone's feelings. People who have taken personality or behavioral-style inventories such as the Myers-Briggs Type Indicator are perhaps particularly aware that some types are highly motivated toward keeping others happy and avoiding conflict. It's a trait that tends to pose an even greater challenge when it's time to deliver criticism.

If your reluctance is so great that it keeps you from approaching the person, just think for a moment about what's happening in the macro picture of the 2M Simultaneous Focus Quick Charge. You are allowing your discomfort to rule. Yet if you truly care about the person and if you know something that could be of benefit to her, then by not saying anything you are denying her an opportunity to improve. If your hesitancy to say anything is caused by a lack of confidence in how best to approach the person, then the following insights and tips might be valuable.

An authoritative psychologist pointed out that because receivers have the control, they are the ones who ultimately allow the words to penetrate, resulting in hurt feelings—even though you had the best of intentions. Because of this perspective, your focus as the giver is to be mindful of the importance of preserving the relationship.

As we've said all along, to help ensure that your message is received as intended, preparation is key. While mentally preparing, factor in everything you know about the receiver, being sure you are able to answer how the receiver prefers being approached, as well as taking into consideration any particular topic or word sensitivities. You also need to be able to answer what's important to the individual. In addition, what are her goals? If you don't know the answers to any of these questions, you may want to delay your message, as the Giver Communication Chart suggests. Also, be sure you have some specific examples to bring up to help provide some substance to your message.

During your mental rehearsal, make sure you select your words carefully (Step III). Take, for example, how a slight modification in your message becomes a probing question, as opposed to a foregone conclusion, when you go from saying, "You don't trust me," to asking, "Is it a matter of trust?" The first statement typically results in a defensive response, but not the second. Likewise, minimize your use of the word "you." In addition, be careful about your tone of voice. It's best to keep it matter-of-fact. Also, pay attention to your facial expressions and your gestures. Since the nonverbal communication of a criticism is a factor that receivers pay close attention to, try to avoid frowning, pointing your finger, raising your voice, or showing anger. These nonverbal signs can send mixed messages. Another effective approach in your delivery is to give the receiver the benefit of the doubt. To avoid coming across as threatening, it's helpful to preface your statements with "You might not be aware" or "Surely, that was not your intent," or even saying something along the lines of "I realize you may have been thinking you were being helpful. . . ." If you deliver the message according to how you see the situation (i.e., your perception) and how it makes you feel, you provide the receiver with some room to respond and present her point of view and engage in a discussion. Be sure during the delivery of your message that you point out the benefit or show what value is to be gained by taking action. In some circumstances, it may result in answering "why" the receiver needs to invest her time and energy.

Here's a sensitive situation that illustrates what we've been discussing. Rich, a fifteen-year seasoned manager, has for the past several years reported to Ellen. Ellen lacks awareness of her strong personality and the fact that she becomes very emotional when confronted. She is determined to succeed and wants the same for all of her direct reports, especially Rich. She thinks he deserves to be promoted. So what's the issue? Ellen delegates tasks to Rich but doesn't let go, and Rich feels like he just comes along for the ride. He's frustrated, discouraged, losing self-confidence, and feeling as if he is not challenged. Besides not wanting to hurt Ellen's feelings, Rich hates getting into conflicts. Even though he's fearful, his frustration level is at an all-time high, so he's willing to risk everything by speaking to Ellen about the issue.

To prepare, Rich is going to make sure that he opens the conversation by framing the discussion around his desire for the two of them to start the new year off right (the meeting is in December). It's also good timing for Ellen; the budgets are in and her schedule isn't as hectic. Now that the stage is set, Rich knows that Ellen likes people to be concise, so he gets right to the point and the conversation unfolds as follows:

> **Rich:** In order to get the new year off to a good start, one thing that would be of great help is to let me be more responsible for the tasks you delegate to me. I don't know if you are aware but with the reconciling of accounts project that you asked me to take on, you were on every teleconference call. *(Rich provides two other specific examples.)* I know you mean well and want me to be promoted. Is it a matter of trust?

> **Ellen:** I had no idea this was an issue for you. I do trust you. How long has this been an issue?

> **Rich:** It's been a while. I haven't said anything until now but for whatever reason, it's really starting to affect my confidence and I felt comfortable enough to bring it up to you. After all, I know you want me to do well. Besides, my taking on these tasks gives you more time to devote to some of the new responsibilities that have been assigned to you. To make sure that you are well informed, I'll give you regular updates.

As it turned out, the conversation was very productive. Rich finally realized that if he didn't say anything, nothing was going to change. If Ellen's feelings were hurt, Rich never knew. All he knows is that the relationship remains intact and that Ellen is backing off when delegating tasks to him. She is allowing him to fight the battles and do what is necessary to complete his tasks. She emphasizes that she is there to support him should he need her help, while at the same time, Rich makes a concentrated effort to keep her up-to-date.

CHALLENGING SITUATION #7:
Your Company Discourages or Bans Use of the Word "Criticism"

There are a growing number of organizations that are banning the use of the word "criticism." In its place they prefer using words like "feedback," "crucial conversations," "coaching moments," or "constructive feedback." These organizations may encounter a problem over time when managers' messages to employees become too generalized and watered down. Nagging issues go unresolved because they are not addressed if there is a chance they will sound too much like criticism. Efficiencies are lost, and productivity begins to suffer. On top of all this, HR departments become overwhelmed with an increasing number of issues that the managers themselves should be addressing. All of this results in a workplace where issues fester and where problematic performers are shifted from one area to another. Besides promoting mediocrity, the murmur of ridicule spreads as managers hide behind the real issues as they relate to poorer performers.

When these conditions exist and you start to hear managers and employees voicing their frustration, then the timing might be right to propose that perhaps an underlying reason for the problems is the lack of understanding of criticism. Explain how a healthy and productive work environment might actually be the result if managers, teams, and employees are willing to offer helpful criticism. Start interjecting "helpful criticism" into your vocabulary when discussing "feedback" or whatever the acceptable word is. See what response you get. Talk to your boss and peers and look to gain their support along the way. Remember to make note of stated organizational values and leadership initiatives that promote transparency and openness, accountability, risk taking, courageousness, and the importance of trust and respect among fellow workers. *Be sure to then explain how criticism is aligned with and supports these initiatives.* Factor in that employees today are far more sophisticated than they were in the past. They know all the leadership buzzwords and, because they are smart, they know when they are being criticized and when they are being coddled—even if the workplace discourages or bans the use of the word "criticism." Look and listen for examples where employees can readily see the doublespeak that exists in the workplace. Examples include the following: "It's okay to be open and transparent, but we can't call things what they are" and "Let's promote accountability—but don't say anything when tasks aren't completed on time or with quality." These are most likely to be only some of the many hypocrisies that employees can readily spot. When they do, the credibility gap widens between the leadership and the employee base. These gaps prohibiting frank interaction need to be addressed before they take hold and eventually corrupt the spirit and integrity of any organization.

Use the proper word: *criticism*. In the English language, there's no real synonym or substitute. What does "feedback" mean? Simply information about what someone did or didn't do. It could be positive or negative. "Praise" has synonyms, but not criticism. Criticism implies a need to change behavior and carries with it real and sometimes imaginary consequences if the desired action isn't taken to remedy the situation. Does your delivery have to include the word "criticism"? Maybe not. But keep in mind that it's no different when coaching someone. Rarely do you hear a coach, trainer, or manager say, "Let me give you some coaching." They typically deliver the nugget of information with a pure expression of helpful criticism.

So be courageous and take a risk by helping those you interact with understand helpful criticism and its value in today's organization.

CHALLENGING SITUATION #8:
Dealing with a Criticism That's Not Correct

Here's a challenging situation. Susan, a production manager, is in a large meeting with her boss, Peter, and Peter's boss, Sam. The purpose of the meeting is to resolve a major problem. There is a lot of back-and-forth discussion between the different parties, and they settle on a course of action. At the conclusion of the meeting, Sam points out to Peter that Susan lacks an ability to think strategically. We all know that it would take a long time to shed a label like this. Susan feels she has been wrongly labeled by Sam. Rather than sit back and complain, she utilizes the control that is inherently hers and takes the following actions.

First, she realizes she has to put herself in situations where others, especially Sam, see her operating strategically. To help her in this effort, Susan goes to Peter to gain his support. Together, they decide that to break Sam's image of Susan, they will refer to her as "the new Susan" in meetings. As Step II of the Giver Communication Chart advises, Peter makes a point of meeting with Sam to find out what Sam is looking for from Susan that would convince Sam that Susan is a leader who can think strategically. Using the insights Peter learns from Sam, he makes sure that Susan is given opportunities to lead certain projects. Besides reporting successes to his boss, Peter invites him to attend meetings that Susan is running. Whenever she needs to address a detailed question, she prefaces it by saying, "I need to revert to my old self where I'm being tactical, but it's necessary, at this moment . . ." and then finishes her sentence.

Having Sam see her operate in action proves extremely helpful. To further strengthen her image as a strategic thinker Peter corrects his boss whenever he makes a reference to Susan as being too tactical. In time, Sam realizes he was in error and judged Susan unfairly.

The takeaways from this example are by no means all-inclusive. But time and time again, taking this kind of action has been shown to be effective. For starters, make sure you get a clear idea of what the giver is looking for from you that would change his image of you. Rephrase what the giver is saying in order to make sure the actions he wants you to take will result in resolving the issue at hand and bring about the desired outcome.

Don't be surprised if you go through this process a few times before everyone understands what the real desired outcome is. A similar dynamic took place with a manager who thought his direct report needed to "improve his interpersonal skills." A purposeful exploration of what the boss was really looking for ensued. It revealed that the desired outcome was for the boss to no longer have to deal with customer complaints from that employee's area. Only when that result was achieved would the boss view his direct report as having "improved his interpersonal skills." Make a point of keeping the truly relevant issue front and center. After all, it's your issue and you need to accept control for doing what you can to change how others perceive you.

Make sure you find or create opportunities where you can be visible so your skills and expertise are clearly displayed. Some people, including bosses, have to see it to believe it! It doesn't hurt to gain the support of others. In Susan's case, she gained the support of her boss, Peter. Any time Peter's boss would make snide remarks about Susan's inability to think strategically, Peter was in there probing his boss and, when appropriate, correcting him. Support also involves having others talk on your behalf to key stakeholders about a success you've achieved. While this isn't always an easy undertaking, it can be achieved and it's your responsibility to drive it.

CHALLENGING SITUATION #9:
Receivers Seem to Indicate Acceptance of the Criticism but Do Nothing About It

When you are dealing with receivers who rarely take any action yet pose themselves as convivial and politely cooperative during a criticism exchange, alarm bells need to go off in your mind. They will signal you to carefully work through Steps II and III of the Giver Communication Chart. A good rule of thumb to follow is this: After a number of attempts to change such a person's behavior with no results on her part, it's time to give consideration to a number of potential conditions. As Step II advises, consider whether your delivery was watered down and softened to the point that the receiver thought your *criticism* was simply *advice* that didn't warrant any action. Perhaps you used the sandwich approach where you started off with a positive, introduced the negative (or criticism), and ended with a positive, and the receiver never heard the criticism because she was rejoicing in the praise part of the dialogue!

When considering Step III, assess whether you are the best person to deliver the criticism to this person. Even though you may be qualified, your message falls on deaf ears. It could be that this is because the receiver views you as powerless and quietly won't accept anything you have to say. Or perhaps the receiver knows that your political or religious views are very different from hers, and it's those differences that result in discrediting whatever you have to say. If you suspect that any such condition might be the case, remember that the end result you are looking for is that the person makes the changes, and you may not be the right one to deliver the message. So find someone else!

There are occasions when a receiver shows great remorse. Realize that a receiver who acts overly apologetic may feel that she is absolved from having to take any action. She may truly believe that your acceptance of her apology equates to wiping the slate clean and requiring no action on her part. Saying "My bad" or "I'm sorry" is fine in the moment, but eventually action needs to be taken to keep the situation from happening again. Many receivers may not make that connection.

Let's take a look back at Step II of the Giver Communication Chart to remind ourselves that there are scenarios in which the receiver doesn't want to change, doesn't know how to change, or is ultimately incapable of changing. When in doubt, as the Giver Communication Chart suggests, probe the receiver. Select a neutral time when nothing negative is going on and casually bring up the subject so that the two of you can explore what's going on and what can be done moving forward. Remember, we are dealing with complex human behavior that most psychiatrists can't even figure out!

CHALLENGING SITUATION #10:
The Receiver Says, "You're Right," but Does Nothing to Correct the Situation

You may encounter a receiver who repeatedly says during the exchange, "You're right." The first time you hear it, you may conclude that the receiver is attempting to be cooperative and is signaling that what you're saying is understood and accepted. However, when no action follows and the two of you are once again having the same or similar conversation, then you want to make a note that when the receiver blurts out, "You're right"—and he will—you now know that it's important to address it by saying that your being right is not the focus of the conversation.

For example, Jim, a direct report of yours, fails to keep you informed. You learn about a problem for the first time during an embarrassing exchange with your boss. You point out the incident to Jim and he immediately says, "You're right." You end the conversation thinking the issue is behind you. Only two weeks later, though, a similar situation arises and you're bringing up the subject again to Jim. Once again, he agrees with you by saying, "You're right." Still giving Jim the benefit of the doubt, you say nothing. However, if the same or similar situation arises again, then this time you need to say something like the following: "The focus of our conversation isn't about who's right. The focus of the conversation is what are you going to do about it." Now you are directing the conversation where it needs to be and you're using criticism as it is intended—to inspire someone to change his behavior.

CHALLENGING SITUATION #11:
The Receiver Says, "Stop Yelling at Me," and You're Not

What about a situation where you are delivering criticism and the receiver says very distinctly, "Stop yelling at me!" You stop talking long enough to assess yourself, and you realize that you are not raising your voice. Then what? Typically, you acknowledge the receiver and say, "I'm not yelling," then continue on with what you have to say, thinking nothing further about the comment

Well, the next time you encounter a similar situation, chances are great that what the receiver is telling you in the unspoken is that your delivery is out of bounds because she is not aware of what she was to do or not to do. So the next time you hear, "Stop yelling at me," take it as an expression that the receiver feels you are making an unjust accusation rather than an attempt to be helpful. When dealing with people who say, "Stop yelling at me," don't make your tone or volume of voice the issue. Rather, move forward by smiling and rephrasing your criticism in helpful language such as: "It's my intention to be helpful, so explain what you mean by saying, 'Stop yelling at me.'" In this way, you both get on the same page and have a greater chance of having a productive conversation.

CHALLENGING SITUATION #12:
The Giver Communication Chart
Does Not Apply

You've most likely concluded, and rightly so, that the Giver Communication Chart no longer applies when you've decided on your own or together with the receiver that the receiver either cannot or will not make the necessary changes. Remember, the sole purpose of delivering criticism is to have the receiver bring about a change in his behavior. If none is possible, then criticism serves no purpose and needs to be aborted. Now you are at the point where you are *counseling* the employee and having discussions about moving him to another area or out of the organization. When you reach this point, you need to make sure you have adequate documentation and the support of your boss, HR, or both.

There are times when we know that a change is necessary but circumstances prevent us from making that move because we need to take steps to get things organized. During these transitional periods, it is key to keep in mind that initiating criticism can lead to an unexpected and damaging outcome that in the end serves little purpose for the giver or others involved.

In a different scenario, what if you elect to keep an employee and let go of the criticism? Imagine you own your own small business and you have a very productive employee, but she regularly comes to work fifteen to twenty minutes late. Each time she's late, you point out how she needs to be on time, but after things improve for a few days, the employee goes back to her old habits. This is what happened to one small-business owner who finally decided to drop the whole matter because, overall, the employee was too valuable to let go. The employee had to handle her kids in the morning, and the issues that would arise were too unpredictable. So instead of getting upset and insisting on her coming to work at the designated starting time, the employer decided to let go of the issue and put up with the tardiness. In the end, both agreed that she would make up the time at the end of the day.

For criticism to be helpful, receivers need to be inspired to change and be capable of making the change. If either of these conditions isn't present, then you need to ask yourself the purpose of continuing to criticize them.

One way to alleviate your frustration and let go of the situation is to recalibrate your expectations and your attitude toward the person. If it's a peer or even a direct report, watch out for getting overinvested in a vision of the individual as you *think* he should behave. Instead, view others as they are and plan your actions according to this different perspective. Who knows? By taking a different attitude and resetting your expectations, you may create a "reverse psychology" situation that leads to the desired behavioral change. It wouldn't be the first time something like that has happened!

Conversations that involve criticism work best when mutual responsibilities and roles are kept in mind. For the giver, it's about making sure you are prepared and thinking before you speak. Your purpose remains in full view and the conversation stays centered on actions the receiver could take to bring about meaningful, valuable, and necessary change. For the receiver, it's recognizing that the control lies with you and what's important is exercising that control. You do that by how you listen, how you inspect information, and how you manage your emotions. What's essential and what's in your control is making sure you have a clear idea of what you need to do moving forward . . . from the giver's perspective!

Keep a big-picture perspective that as long as you are working, interacting with others, and striving to learn and do better, you can't escape criticism. Sure, the truth hurts, but it's what you do with the information that turns the initial hurt into something that propels you forward, feeling empowered along the way.

When givers and receivers utilize the skills introduced in this book, relationships are strengthened because there is a fostering of trust and respect. Performance is enhanced and consistent results are achieved. These are skills you can use and benefit from for the rest of your life, wherever you go and with whomever you interact.

Quick Review for Easy Recall

Here are some challenging situations for givers and responses to those challenges:

- ► The receiver has low vocabulary skills: Ask the receiver to repeat back to you what corrective action she is expected to take.

- ► The receiver starts to cry: Exit the room.

- ► The receiver tends to blow up: Be sure you can explain why the criticism is inbounds.

- ► The heat of the conversation is escalating: Stop talking and politely ask if it's possible to "hit the reset button" or postpone the discussion.

- ► The situation is unusual or difficult: First consider if it is urgent then whether your criticism is within bounds.

- ► Another person's feelings might be hurt: Take particular care to grasp how the receiver prefers being approached, what's important to him, and what his goals are.

► The receiver agrees with the criticism or says, "You're right": Be sure that action on the part of the receiver follows.

Here are some challenging situations for receivers and responses to those challenges:

► Givers don't know what it is they want: Play back to them what you think they want you to do, and break larger tasks into smaller parts sent to them for approval on completion.

► Givers criticize unfairly: Take the initiative to set the record straight.

The Giver Communication Chart is used only when receivers can bring about a change in their behavior. If none is possible, then the Giver Communication Chart no longer applies. Now it's a counseling session to move the employees or guide them out of the organization.

Notes

INTRODUCTION

1. Bob Kelly, *Worth Repeating: More Than 5,000 Classic and Contemporary Quotes* (Grand Rapids, MI: Kregel Academic, 2003), 273.

CHAPTER 1:
Criticism Doesn't Have to Hurt

1. Nicholas Fernandez, *The Man I Always Knew: A True Story of Faith, Family and Honor* (Xlibris Corporation, 2010), 95.

2. Dale Carnegie, *How to Win Friends and Influence People* (New York: Simon & Schuster, 1936), 5.

3. Bright Enterprises and Penelope Boehm, *Criticism Survey*, September 2013. Unpublished survey.

CHAPTER 2:
Criticism Manners:
Common Mistakes, and Some Dos and Don'ts

1. Mokokoma Mokhonoana, "Aphorisms," http://www.mokokoma.com/aphorisms/ (accessed April 28, 2014).

2. Bright Enterprises and Technometrica, *Strategies for Enhancing Performance Initiative 2003–2011*, 2011. Unpublished study.

3. Deborah Bright, *Criticism in Your Life: How to Give It, How to Take It, How to Make It Work for You* (New York: Master Media Ltd., 1990), 26.

4. Robert A. Baron, "Negative Effects of Destructive Criticism: Impact on Conflict, Self-Efficacy, and Task Performance," *Journal of Applied Psychology*, 73(2) (May 1988): 199–207.

5. Sue Shellenbarger, "When the Boss Is a Screamer," *Wall Street Journal*, August 15, 2012.

6. Daniel Goleman, "Why Job Criticism Fails: Psychology's New Findings," *New York Times*, July 26, 1988.

7. *Strategies for Enhancing Performance Initiative*.

8. Deborah Bright and Anita Crockett, "Training Combined with Coaching Can Make a Significant Difference in Job Performance and Satisfaction," *Coaching: An International Journal of Theory, Research and Practice*, 5(1) (March 2012): 4–21.

9. Peggy Anderson, comp., *Great Quotes from Great Leaders* (Lombard, IL: Successories® Publishing, 1990), 21.

10. K. Anders Ericsson, Michael J. Prietula, and Edward T. Cokely, "The Making of an Expert," *Harvard Business Review*, 85(7–8) (July–August 2007: 114-21.

CHAPTER 3:
Creating an Atmosphere of Acceptance: Establish Clear
Relationship Expectations

1. Criss Jami, "Mission: Impossible Briefing," May 13, 2011. http://the killosopher.blogspot.com/2011/05/in-nutshell-and-on-go.html (accessed April 28, 2014).

2. Paul Campos, "Viewpoint: Chris Christie's Weight Isn't a Big Issue," *Time*, February 8, 2013.

3. Deborah Bright, *Criticism in Your Life: How to Give It, How to Take It, How to Make It Work for You* (New York: Master Media, Ltd., 1990), 223.

CHAPTER 4:
Delivering Criticism with Confidence in Sensitive Times

1. Houston Mitchell, "John Wooden Quotes: Some of Coach John Wooden's Favorite Maxims ('Woodenisms')," *Los Angeles Times*, June 4, 2010.

2. Bright Enterprises, *Criticism in the Workplace Survey*, December, 2013. Unpublished survey.

CHAPTER 5:
Receiving Criticism: You Have More Control Than You Think

1. Peter Archer, *The Quotable Intellectual: 1,417 Bon Mots, Ripostes, and Witticisms for Aspiring Academics, Armchair Philosophers . . . and Anyone Else Who Wants to Sound Really Smart* (Avon, MA: Adams Media, 2010), 129.

2. Daniel Frezza, "About the Playwright: George Bernard Shaw," 2007. http://www.bard.org/Education/studyguides/candida/candidaplaywright.html (accessed February 12, 2008).

3. Steve Maraboli, *Life, the Truth, and Being Free* (Port Washington, NY: A Better Today Publishing, 2009).

4. M. I. Seka, *Life Lessons of Wisdom and Motivation: Insightful, Enlightened and Inspirational Quotations and Proverbs (Volume 2)* (Phoenix, AZ: Providential Press, 2014), 254.

CHAPTER 6:
Avoiding the Tendency to Personalize Criticism

1. Eleanor Roosevelt II, *With Love, Aunt Eleanor: Stories from My Life with the First Lady of the World* (Scrapbook Press, 2004), 73.

2. Deborah Bright and Anita Crockett, "Training Combined with Coaching Can Make a Significant Difference in Job Performance and Satisfaction," *Coaching: An International Journal of Theory, Research and Practice*, 5(1) (March 2012): 4–21.

3. Matt Ehalt, "Report Frustrates Jets' Tim Tebow," *ESPN New York*, November 15, 2012. http://espn.go.com/new-york/nfl/story/_/id/8633241/tim-tebow-new-york-jets-frustrated-sad-criticism-report (accessed December 13, 2013).

4. Nicholas Tavuchis, "Mea Culpa: A Sociology of Apology and Reconciliation," in *Work, Youth, and Schooling: Historical Perspectives on Vocationalism in American Education*, Harvey Kantor and David Tyack, eds. (Stanford, CA: Stanford University Press, 1982), 5.

5. Richard S. Gallagher, *How to Tell Anyone Anything: Breakthrough Techniques for Handling Difficult Conversations at Work* (New York: AMACOM, 2009).

6. Johnny Bench. Interview by author. Early 1990s.

CHAPTER 7:
Managing Work and Volunteer Teams:
The Crucial Role Criticism Plays

1. Yogi Berra, *You Can Observe a Lot by Watching: What I've Learned About Teamwork from the Yankees and Life* (New York: John Wiley & Sons, 2009), 186.

2. Charlan Nemeth et al., "The Liberating Role of Conflict in Group Creativity: A Cross-Cultural Study," *European Journal of Social Psychology*, 34 (2004): 365–74.

3. David Burkus, "Why Fighting for Our Ideas Makes Them Better," *99U*. http://99u.com/articles/7224/Why-Fighting-For-Our-Ideas-Makes-Them-Better.

4. Jack Zenger and Joseph Folkman, "The Ideal Praise-to-Criticism Ratio," *Harvard Business Review Blog Network*, March 15, 2013. http://blogs.hbr.org/2013/03/the-ideal-praise-to-criticism/.

CHAPTER 8:
Handling Difficult Situations

1. Gene N. Landrum, *The Innovative Mind: Stop Thinking, Start Being* (Garden City, NY: Morgan James Publishing, 2008), 177.

2. Harvey Chipkin, "Hotels Putting Increased Emphasis on Customer Service," *Travel Weekly*, May 23, 2006. http://www.travelweekly.com/Travel-News/Hotel-News/Hotels-putting-increased-emphasis-on-customer-service/.

Index